INVESTITUDE

(Name Given to this bo

Presented To:

Presented By:

Date:

INVESTITUDE

By

Juan Phillip Chisholm

First Edition: October 2008
Second Edition: March 2019
Third Edition: December 2020

Green Light Books & Publishing, LLC
P.O. Box 1965
Orlando, Florida 32802-1965
www.GreenlightBooks.org
Book Orders: Info@greenlightbooks.org

www.Investitude.com
www.YoungInvestors.org
www.JuanChisholm.com

Published by Juan Phillip Chisholm

ISBN: 978097551105

INVESTITUDE

By

Juan Phillip Chisholm

Dedication

In loving memory of Mr. Eugene & Mrs. Alnora Rebecca Chisholm:

Thank you dad and mom for believing in me, teaching me the power of positive self-esteem, always trusting me to do what's best, and sharing so many impactful lessons with me that I continue to grow from and share with so many others.

You are and will continue to be forever in my heart as I continue the legacy that you shared with me.

- JPC

About the Author

Dr. Juan P. Chisholm is an acclaimed business owner, investor, author, and motivational speaker. He has successfully completed the world-renown Executive Education program in Strategic Finance at the Harvard Business School in Boston. He is the published author of two financial books: *Investitude* and *How To Make Your Past, A Blessing To Your Future*. He was featured in an exclusive interview in Black Enterprise® Magazine, the premiere wealth-building resource for African Americans. He is also the Founder of Young Investors, Inc., a non-profit that educates young adults regarding financial literacy and investment strategy and has chapters throughout the United States.

Dr. Juan P. Chisholm is also a proud graduate of Florida State University (FSU). While attending FSU, he majored in English Literature and minored in Business, Economics and Black Studies. He was elected FSU's Homecoming King and was also elected College Brother of the Year of Alpha Phi Alpha Fraternity, Inc. After graduating from Florida State University, he earned his law degree from Florida A&M University College of Law in Orlando, Florida where he was the two-time recipient of the prestigious Percy R. Luney Spirit of Service Award.

Dr. Juan P. Chisholm is active in the community. He serves on the Board of Directors of Revolution

Leadership®, Inc. (www.RevolutionLeadership.org), a national non-profit organization that awards college scholarships and serves students nationwide. He is active in his local church and is the founder of American Nation Builders College Preparatory Academy (www.AmericanNationBuilders.org).

Dr. Juan P. Chisholm is happily married to his wife and best-friend, Attorney Audrey K. Chisholm. They reside in the beautiful city of Orlando, Florida and are parents of three beautiful daughters.

www.JuanChisholm.com

Acknowledgements

I thank you God for being my guiding light and inspiration. Without you Lord, this seed would not be planted.

Also, I thank you for the wonderful and loving friend that you have given me through my wife Audrey. I now understand what it means and feels like to have my other half make me feel complete. Thank you for all of your love, help, support and patience as your author was finding his inspiration for Investitude. I love you.

To my grandmother, I love you. Thank you for being my biggest fan and most loyal supporter. Also, thank you for always telling me how proud you are. Your affirmation and love means a great deal.

Mom and Dad, thank you for always being so supportive of me and reminding me to take care of business. Thank you for your love, support, and prayers.

To my second mom and dad (and Ms. Turner), thank you for making me laugh and welcoming me inside your hearts. Also, thank you for having reared up such a strong and wonderful woman of God to call my wife. I love and appreciate all of you. To Carlos,

Jason, James, Carlos II, Jade, Alice, and Amanda – you all are loved very much.

Lastly, to my friends, extended family and readers, thank you for sharing another adventure with me. Also, thank you all for helping send me to Harvard. I hope you find this one is even more interesting than the first. And a special thank you to my friends, Tarsha Thomas, Marcus Johnson and Ms. Delia Winston for all of your love and prayers.

I thank you again God for opening my eyes to brighter days. And to the readers of this book, I pray that these chapters of my life will be a blessing unto you.

Love,

Juan.

Foreword

When God gave me the vision to write, *Investitude,* he told me that "It is time to become, who you are destined to be." I excitedly scribbled this phrase down on the first sheet of paper I could find. Then, as I was led to *glance* at that paper again, after again, and after again, I became irritated and doubtful because I realized that at that moment in my life, I felt that achieving this vision would be impossible because I had been caught in the middle of a spiritual storm. But, that's when the Holy Spirit would constantly re-affirm me through the Lord's life-breathing *words* of affirmation that "It is time to become, who I am destined to be."

I trusted God's Words for my life and pressed towards the mark despite my flesh and was delivered from my storm. There, I was able to rest and in a place of peace; everything remaining from the storm was now Beautiful, and I was able to appreciate the Lord's faithfulness and what He had carried me through.

Through that particular testimony in my life, I believe that it all had to happen in order to unlock blessings for my family members, friends, and students; and successfully bring unbelievers to Christ. God also used that testimony to channel me in a new career. I re-entered school to pursue a J.D., purchased a new home, and I am now married to my lovely wife, Mrs. Audrey K. Chisholm, J.D. What I learned from this experience is to continue to trust God in the mist of the storms of your life, for His direction and through His direction, God revealed that you become who you are destined to be. I pray that this nugget from my life helps you to reaching your potential/promised land and encourages you to believe that your time is here and "It's time to become, who you are destined to be."

Table of Contents

Unit Three: X-Factors

Unit Four: Entrepreneurship

Unit Five: Investing

INVESTITUDE

UNIT ONE: INVESTITUDE

Chapter I

Investitude

Investitude

"No one can go back and make a brand new start, my friend, but anyone can start from here and make a brand new end."

Anonymous

Home: Heart, Mind, and Soul.
Please, Park Here First.

Investitude, in a nutshell is about teaching you *how to think, see, organize, and work with the financial resources, gifts, and opportunities that you already have* in order to achieve your financial goals and find success. This can be achieved **without** aimlessly working a second or third job; taking a second mortgage to make ends meet; living off of a line of credit; missing out on precious moments with family members and friends; and not having valuable personal time to pursue your travel dreams, life goals, or other important aspirations. Investitude is designed to help you draft a solid financial game plan, build and better manage your current wealth, and further enhance your financial position and place in life. These goals are accomplished by making strategic financial decisions in the areas of your residual income, x-factors, entrepreneurship, and investing. The powerful financial principles that you will learn from these key areas will greatly impact your financial future and life.

Unit One will first introduce you to the life-changing concept of Spirituality and Wealth. These timeless principles will set the foundation for your journey to having the right Investitude. This unit will also teach you to be more cognizant of the small decisions that you make due to their impact on your life and financial future. In addition, you will be introduced to eight small decisions you can make immediately that will improve your financial situation.

Unit Two will address the contours of Residual Income. This unit will feature chapters on budgeting your finances; identifying your financial position; assessing your net worth; reaching short-term and long-term goals; finding out about part-time jobs that offer full-time benefits; and numerous others. As a result of reading this unit on residual income, you will be better equipped with the necessary tools to be the best steward of your income and able to confidently advance your financial position to new heights.

Next, in Unit Three, Investitude will help you find and use your **X-Factors.** X-Factors are God given gifts, creative talents, and other abilities that you possess that have the potential to positively impact your community and world-at-large when properly utilized. Moreover, Investitude will show you how you can rely on these gifts to earn additional income on your own time without engaging in unethical or illegal activities. Some of the chapters covered in this unit will feature insight on using your X-Factor to earn additional income; finding and operating in your calling; climbing the wall to reaching your X-Factor; earning money while finding inner-peace; how to juggle extra-curricular activities with family; and more. As a result of reading this unit on X-Factors, you will be able to take advantage of the opportunities that have always been in front of you. In addition, you will know how to earn money while doing something that you enjoy.

Fourthly, in Unit Four, Investitude will prove to you that you have the heart of an effective **entrepreneur** by encouraging you to push your X-Factor to its maximum potential and turn it into an income producing business. In this unit, Investitude will assist you in positioning your business for success through helpful chapters on managing, enhancing, and gradually building your business. Some of the chapters covered in this unit will feature lessons on the following areas: how to become an effective entrepreneur; writing your business plan; how to build and maintain your business; how to use the Small Business Association as a point of contact and place of reference; becoming an expert; business growing techniques and strategies; and others. After reading this unit, you will be ready to achieve your personal goal of business ownership and experience the rewards of being an effective entrepreneurship.

Finally, in Unit Five, Investitude will help you to strategically place and increase your saved dollars through superb money management growing techniques in unit four on *Investments*. Some of the topics covered will include: High-Yield Saving Accounts, IRAs, 401Ks, Home Ownership, and others. After reading this unit, you will be able to confidently understand the available venues that you can invest your money in as well as recognize the benefits and pitfalls associated with each one. In sum, this chapter will help you to make your investment experience an informed one.

Once you have completed this final chapter on investing, I strongly recommend that you purchase a copy of my first book: How To Make Your Past, A Blessing To Your Future (ISBN: 0-0755110-0-9). It's a comprehensive book that will introduce you to other investment vehicles such as saving bonds, certificates of deposits (CDs), stocks, mutual funds, real estate, investment clubs, wills, and others. The book also includes long-term and short-term investment plans and practical investment strategies that will help you to further put the financial principles into action. Copies are available at: www.JuanChisholm.com.

6 Reading Rules of Investitude

These Six Rules of Investitude are designed to help guide your reading experience. I pray that these rules are able to add to your reading by making it fun, easy, and interactive.

Rule # 1: Name Me!

Return back to the front (index) pages and give your Investitude book a reputable name. This was done to establish a relationship between you and your Investitude book. My prayer is that the relationship is a long-term one that will bless you indeed.

Rule # 2: Write in me!

Write in me! Write in me! Write in me! You have my permission to write in me. This writing may also include underlining, highlighting, circling, and all other types of markings. The goal in asking that you *write in me* is to provide you with all necessary means to help you achieve the financial success that you deserve. So let's make it easy, you may write in me.

Rule #3: Use your License to Jump or Power Drive.

Through the course of your reading, rule # 3 gives you the option to either *Jump* (skip around) or

Power Drive (read straight through). Therefore, if you choose to Power-Drive, you are reading Investitude in a linear direction (i.e. chapters 1, 2, 3…23) or you may choose to Jump, which means that you have decided to read by *skipping around* (i.e. from Chapter One up to Chapter Twenty-Three, then move *back* to Chapter Seven and finally return back to Chapter One). It is also okay if you randomly Jump some chapters and Power-Drive others. Please take advantage of the method that works best for you. Also, if you do decide to Jump around, you may find the Table of Contents helpful in directing you to the place that you want to land.

Rule #4: Visit www.Investitude.com.

Take advantage of all the resources available at www.Investitude.com. This website is designed to provide you with valuable financial tools and resources that will help you to achieve your financial goals. Please put these resources to work by using them and recommending them to your friends. They were made to become apart of your everyday life, reading, financial health, and success to move you in the right Investitude! Please take full advantage of www.Investitude.com.

Rule #5: Share with Others.

Share Investitude with others. If you liked the concepts or enjoyed the materials, please feel free to share it with your family members, church members, friends, colleagues, and other people you associate with. This book makes a great gift for birthdays, weddings and graduations. Also, encourage them to purchase their own copy of Investitude!

Rule #6: Use the Investitude Glossary.

Various financial terms are included throughout the text and can be looked up in the Investitude Glossary at the end of the text. All of the words that are in bold lettering are defined via this glossary as well as a few others that are generally common to the subject matter of Investitude. The glossary can be found at the end of the book. If you need more assistance in finding a term that is not found in Investitude, please visit our web site for more resources and links to financial dictionaries.

Apply these six rules while you are reading Investitude. They will help guide your reading and make it a more rewarding experience. Enjoy!

Is this book for me?

This book is *not* for you if **one** you can go through life without ever worrying about money. **Two**, if there's not at least one person on this planet that you have ever cared or will ever care about in the future. **Three**, if you do not want a solid financial future. If these 3 statements apply to your life, then I love you and I'll especially send a prayer out for you.

But if you are like most of us, and in disagreement with these statements, then allow us to begin to hold hands spiritually, mentally, intellectually, and financially as we prepare to journey together and learn collectively, what it means to have the right Investitude!

Chapter II

Spirituality & Wealth

Spirituality & Wealth

"What good will it be for a man if he gains the whole world, yet forfeits his soul? Or what can a man give in exchange for his soul?"

Matthew 16:26 (NIV)

How do you define success? For some people, defining success could have various meanings. Success could mean having a lot of money, achieving one's personal goals or aspirations, opening up a business, being committed to the same employer or person for a number of years, giving birth and/or raising healthy children, having grandchildren, being happy, and/or teaching someone something new. All of these things can be encompassed inside the sacred and precious box that holds our definition of success or what it means to be successful. Do you also find yourself agreeing or looking to add more to this definition? There is one thing that is not mentioned and is often times overlooked when it comes to being successful. And that one thing does not negate the other meanings of success. The one thing that should determine our success and be the guiding percept of our life is being obedient to God. This is what I believe to be the true definition of success.

The Christian Bible tells us a lot of things on obedience and that obedience to God is not just paying a tithe. Instead, obedience to God is being in tune with the voice of the Lord and knowing it as if it was your mother, father, parent, or other guardian. It is that same voice that may ask you to sacrifice some of the things and people that you love in order to become one step closer to Him and become successful. It is that same obedience that will challenge you to learn that sometimes when you are facing the toughest days, most challenging moments and life circumstances, and the world seems like it is against you, that as long as you hold firm to God and what He told you to do, it is better than being in a place with one million dollars but outside of His will. Someone close to me often reminds me that "The worst place in God's will is better than the best place outside of it." So, my challenge to you with *Investitude* is for you to view success, not just as having money, high position, achieving goals, opening up a business, and being dedicated to your employer, but to be obedient to God in whatever He may ask of you to do—for better or for what you believe is worst—be obedient to God.

And through your obedience and living a holy lifestyle, I believe that God will ultimately open up more doors of success for your obedience juxtaposed to more doors being opened to you for striving to be a success. So, the next time the question is presented: How do you define success? Allow your words, thoughts, and actions to say "obedience to God" and allow it to be the guiding precept to your success here on earth, which will pay you the ultimate compensation in heaven. I pray that this insight from me has been able to be a blessing unto you.

Chapter III

The Choices <u>You</u> Make, Define Who <u>You</u> Are

The Choices You Make, Define Who You Are

"Small decisions can greatly impact your life." — Juan Phillip Chisholm

Small Decision. Big Impact. One of the best experiences of my life was when I applied for admission to Florida State University in Tallahassee, Florida. I was rejected several times. A small decision to drive up to Tallahassee, Florida from Jacksonville, Florida (a 2 hour drive) after school one day and knock on the doors of the admission officers at Florida State University changed this gray cloud of defeat into hope. There, I met with one lady that had worked so intimately with my file that she was familiar with me from my paperwork. When I mentioned my first name, she quickly recognized that I had been the person on her voicemail that had been respectfully asking for appeal after appeal of their admissions decision. She said to me, "We [the Office of Admission] have made our decision on your behalf and you have *not* been accepted by Florida State." I responded by saying, "While that's what your letters said, I drove up here hoping that you would meet again to make one final decision on my behalf." She reluctantly agreed only after making me promise that I would move on with my life regardless of their final decision.

After standing outside her door for about 15 minutes, the admission officer returned. In her hand was a small folded note. When I opened it, it had four simple words: "Welcome to Florida State!" My face lit up. I had been denied by several smaller colleges and yet, God had blessed me to be accepted into my number one University of choice. This small decision to drive to Tallahassee changed my life! Despite how rough the road was to be admitted, once I was enrolled as a student there, I was blessed to have won two major awards and received one mega distinction. The two major awards that I won were 1) the Alpha Phi Alpha Fraternity, Incorporated College Brother of the Year Award (for Florida) and 2) I was the 2004 FSU Homecoming King. Lastly, I published my first book. All of these were the result of one small decision that obviously had a big impact on my life. For me, the small decision was knocking on the admission officer's door that had told me "No!" The big impact was graduating from my number one college of choice, and the accomplishments that ensued.

* * *

Do you believe that the choices you make define who you are? Or, more plainly stated, will the decisions you make today determine where you may ultimately end up in life? Well, I believe it to be a fact that the choices you make today will ultimately determine where you will end up in life. Through this portion of Investitude, we will focus on the significance of small decisions involving money to show you what a great impact that making these small decisions can have on your financial life.

8 Small Decisions that Make a Big Impact!

Here are 8 small decisions that will have a major impact on your financial life. If you have already completed any of these items, then please put a check inside the small box beside the item in order to document your accomplishment of completing it. Remember Rule # 2, you can *write in me*!

❑ 1. Open up a bank account!

This will help you to save and better track your money. There is also a correlation between the more money you immediately have in your pocket(s) at any given time and the money that you spend. Simply put, this means that the more money people have at their discretion in their pockets, the more they are likely to spend. Thus, by putting your money aside in your bank account, this may save you from spending unnecessarily or unplanned amounts, which will help you to save more money. Please be advised to find a financial institution that allows you to open a bank account for free and does not have any hidden bank charges. Also, be sure to request a debit card (not a credit card). For more on credit cards, please read the *Conversation with the Author* at the end of this chapter.

❑ 2. Save your receipts

Start saving your receipts. This can be a very helpful practice when it comes to managing and maintaining your finances. By getting in the habit of saving receipts, it will also allow you to track your spending habits from your day-to-day spending activities. You will also be able to use them to deduct certain business expenses as tax write-offs in the event that you decide to utilize the principles in Unit 4 and become an entrepreneur.

❑ 3. Create a budget

Use the *Investitude Budgeting Worksheet* in Chapter 5 to create a budget. This will help you to become an even better steward of your income and financial resources. This chart will assist you in learning how to budget your finances and applying that budget to your day-to-day activities.

❑ 4. Start to save money for yourself as if you are paying a bill

Pressure yourself to start to save money for yourself as if you are paying a bill. Moreover, discipline yourself to save at least a consistent amount or percentage each month (i.e. like *$100.00* or *33%* of your earnings from each pay period, or some other amount). Also, whatever amount you start to put aside, continue to gradually increase it over time. In addition, please note that it is a healthy practice to give yourself small, positive rewards when you accomplish your monthly or yearly financial goals of saving money. Some of these personal rewards could be as simple as going to the movies with friends or taking a *planned* vacation. Please make sure that you budget for whatever your reward is for yourself.

❑ 5. Put a dollar away a day for other investments.

As an alternative to # 4, try putting a dollar away a day or dollars away each week for other investments. This is a simple financial strategy that will help you to set and achieve daily or weekly financial goals by setting a small amount of money aside to be applied towards other investments. This process can be as simple as planning to save $3.25 a day or $22.75 each week. Initially, this money can be put aside in a small *piggy bank,* but when it reaches a certain amount, the goal is to move it from the *piggy* and put it towards an investment vehicle(s). Please see Unit Five on Investing and purchase a copy of my first book for more detailed information on the specific investment venues available for you. For now, put the money aside and put it in your piggy bank.

❑ 6. Start an emergency fund!

If you don't have an **emergency fund**, start one! Please note that emergency funds are usually 3-5 months of income saved or invested conservatively based on your immediate bills and life expenses for emergency use only. For example, if your bills and life expenses total $1,000 per month, then your emergency fund should be between $3,000-$5,000. Please be sure to separate the money you use for spending, saving, and/or investing from your emergency fund money.

❑ 7. Become A Giver!

Giving is a true sign of success! If there were no givers, many of us would not even be close to where we are today. When you learn to give back and give to others, it will always come back to you. Try giving and trust that God will give it back to you.

❑ 8. Pay Tithes to God.

Trusting God with your money can be one of the most challenging things that you can do with your finances. But, once you understand its significance and try it by giving your finances to Him, it is one of the most fulfilling and rewarding things that you could ever do with your finances. The reason you should tithe (giving 10% of your income) to God is not to give to Him in expectation of getting something back in return. Instead, when you tithe, you are acknowledging that the reason that you have is *because God gave it to you.* In addition, it solidifies the bond that He is your Father and you are his children and servants; and through this bond, He has protected you, provided for you, and through Him, your life has been reconnected to its true purpose. This is the significance of the tithe. The tithe represents the 10% of your earnings that you should willingly give *back* to God. So try it, not for little me, but for a great, mighty, powerful, and magnificent God.

If you have been successful in achieving these initial goals of Investitude, I congratulate you! Job well done! However, if you have not achieved all of these initial goals, then I encourage you to continue to strive to do so and work towards the objective of checking off all eight. Moreover, by accomplishing these initial, small financial decisions, they will greatly impact your life and help you to work towards the goal of having *the right Investitude.* I pray that this insight from me has been able to be a blessing unto you.

<u>A Conversation with the Author:</u>

The Impact of Making One Small Decision: Credit Cards

Am I against credit cards? No. However what I am against is the way that credit cards are used to financially knock so many people out and set so many people back.

Although one small decision, like applying to college or implementing one of the steps in this chapter can change your life, making one poor decision can also ruin it. Moreover, the type of poor decision that I am referring to happens all the time when it comes to making the decision to either accept or *trash* that innocent, little piece of plastic that we call **credit cards**. Interestingly, credit cards appear to be very appealing. They offer users shopping discounts and travel incentives while parading the message that *having a credit card will make your life worry free* (about money) and help you to establish credit. They are also easy to get, easy to use, and easy to *charge.* It's just that easy!

However, it's that same easy nature and simplicity that becomes the problem that plagues so many credit card users and causes them to either swim or drown in credit card debt and cry for financial help. This could be the result of underestimating the impact of taking that innocent, little piece of plastic. And it gets worst! Credit cards often either fail to tell or credit users fail to understand the importance of the interest rate of the credit cards. If that little, innocent piece of plastic was a boxer, understand that the higher the interest rate (between 20%-40%), the more damage that little piece of plastic will cost you each time you step in the ring with it by using it. Alternatively, if the credit card offers a lower interest rate (10% or less), that innocent, credit card will still punch you - just not as severely as the higher one - each time you step in the ring with it by using it. But, here's the reality check: How many people enjoy being the punching bag of anything? Surely, not I. So, why settle and become the punching bag of a credit card?

Also, whereas a credit card could be used to establish credit history, there are other alternatives available to help you to establish credit without a credit card. Here are five ways to establish credit without using a credit card.

5 Ways to Establish Credit without a Credit Card

1. Maintaining a bank account.
2. Paying a bill in your name (i.e. phone bill or a utility bill).
3. Having a stable employment history.
4. Living at the same place of residence.
5. Getting a co-signer (i.e. a parent or guardian).

All of these ways can be used to establish credit without a credit card. These 5 ways can be used to prove to your lender that you are worthy of being approved for a loan in order to secure financing for a home mortgage, car, or other purpose. Also, if you are a parent and looking for other ways to teach your children about money without using a credit card, please see *Chapter 10: Allowances*. I pray that this insight from me has been able to be a blessing unto you.

Unit Two: Residual Income

Chapter IV

Residual Income

Residual Income

"Success lies not in being the best, but in doing your best." Anonymous

Payday! One of the happiest days for most people (next to birthdays, holidays, and anniversaries) is their payday. This is one of the special days where you are saluted with monetary compensation in honor of what you have done or the services you have rendered. And whether it comes to you in the form of cash, check, money order, through an online transfer to your bank, or all of the above, your payday is definitely something to celebrate. Because while every other day is seen as Monday, Tuesday, Wednesday, Thursday, Friday, Saturday, and Sunday; this day is different—"It's payday!"

All forms of compensation received on your payday are considered a portion of what makes up your **residual income**. Your total residual income is the total amount of money that you actually receive over a year's time. This can be a very powerful number because knowing what it is gives you the *power of choice* and may help you to establish your **personal net worth**. The power of choice allows you to decide on the size of your home, the neighborhood you live in, the car you drive, the business that you are able to start or purchase, and when retirement is a realistic goal among others. Through this unit on

Residual Income, Investitude will help you to increase this number and as a result expand your power of choice by helping you to become a better steward of your finances and helping you to allocate them accordingly.

In addition, what you will learn in this Unit is that the power of choice is not just reserved for the rich, famous, and affluent. Instead, it is solely dependant upon how much of your residual income you are able to put away into saving and investment venues. In other words, if you don't make as much as you would like, but you are able to strategically save and invest more of your residual income, you can acquire the same power of choice that is traditionally granted to people who may in fact make more money than you. Now that's encouraging! We will discuss specific venues for saving and investing in more detail in Unit Five on Investing. Now, let's get started on discovering strategic ways of increasing your residual income.

What Is Residual Income?

Residual Income is having steady sources of income that you can count on to determine how much money you actually make. Most people consider the more prominent sources of residual income to include:

- A steady paycheck

- ❑ A guaranteed planned bonus check (e.g., Christmas bonus check or an incentive bonus payout check for an accomplishment, etc.)
- ❑ A profit (net earnings) from being self-employed.
- ❑ A commission check
- ❑ Income from a rental property
- ❑ Interest Income from investments
- ❑ ________________
- ❑ ________________
- ❑ ________________
- ❑ ________________
- ❑ ________________

All of these are forms of Residual Income. Go ahead and check the ones that you are receiving! If there were others that were not included, please write them in the blank spaces above and include them as your residual income.

How can I calculate my Residual Income?

In order to calculate your residual income, here are some of the various ways:

Option #1: Calculating *Monthly* Residual Income

Take the total amount you make in a year and divide it by the number 12 (The number 12 represents the total number of months in a year). This amount equals your monthly Residual Income. Now let's walk through the process together.

<u>Step 1:</u>
Write in the total amount you make here:

____

<u>Step 2:</u>
Divide the number you wrote down in step one by "12". Remember that 12 represents the number of months in a year.

<u>Step 3</u>
Write down the number you received as an outcome for following step two below:

____

This amount equals your monthly Residual Income.

Option #2: Calculating Bi-*Weekly* Residual Income

Take the amount that equaled your monthly Residual Income. Divide that number by 2 (The number 2 represents the number of biweekly pay periods usually in a month). This amount equals your weekly Residual Income. Now let's walk through the process!

<u>Step 1:</u>

Write in the total amount you made as monthly Residual Income below:

____

Step 2:
Divide the number you wrote down in step one by "2". Remember that "2" usually represents the two biweekly pay periods in each month.

Step 3:
Write down the number you received as a result for following step two below:

____

This amount equals your bi-weekly Residual Income.

Option #3: Calculating *Weekly* Residual Income

Take the amount that equaled your monthly Residual Income. Divide that number by 4 (The number 4 represents four weeks out of a month). This amount equals your weekly Residual Income. Now let's walk through the process!

Step 1:
Write in the total amount you made as monthly Residual Income below:

____

Step 2:

Divide the number you wrote down in step one by "4". Remember that "4" represents the number of weeks usually in a month.

Step 3:
Write down the number you received as a result for following step two below:

____

This amount equals your weekly Residual Income.

These are some of the numerous ways to calculate your residual income. Plug in your amounts to know just how much you make.

How can I increase my residual income and increase my choices?

Time, Discipline, and Strategically position myself.

There are three common links between residual income and increasing your power of choice. They are linked through the concepts of **Financial Stewardship**, **Financial Discipline**, and **Strategically Positioning Yourself** with your financial goals in mind.

1. Financial Stewardship

Financial Stewardship is best bought to life in keeping track of your money. This is simply being cognizant of where your money is going. This will not only allow you to keep track of you finances, but it will help prevent you from being cheated by stores since you will actually review your receipts to confirm that you have been charged proper amounts for your expenses.

Keeping track of your finances can also be easily achieved by:

1. **Keeping a receipt pouch**. Use a zip lock bag, legal sized envelope, or other storage box to hold all of your original receipts. Review them on a regular basis to ensure that you were accurately billed for purchases.

2. **Keep an expense journal.**
   Buy a spiral bound notebook and list your expenses each month. Don't estimate but write specific amounts so that you can know exactly where you are spending your money. For those who are more technologically savvy, you can create a Microsoft Excel Spreadsheet or just generate a Word Document in which you list your expenses. You simply want to list the name of the company you purchased from and the amount of the item.

By following these techniques of better tracking your spending habits, it will translate into making you a more cautious spender and overall better steward of your finances. For more information on items to help track your receipts, please visit: www.Investitude.com.

2. Financial Discipline

In order to create a financial plan and stick to it, it requires *financial disciplin*e. Financial discipline is simply setting a financial goal (i.e. $10,000 dollars saved per year) and putting the time, energy, and resources towards achieving your goal. In this plan, you can determine, just how much you would like to save and invest in order to make it work best for you. This can be as simple as mandating yourself to save a certain amount (i.e. $500 or 50%) of each pay check or form of income that you receive. Please be realistic in your planning to determine just how much you can do without hurting yourself or your family.

Moreover, the future benefit in having financial discipline is great! You make an immediate financial sacrifice today, which enables you to have more options in your future. These future benefits are often accomplished by applying the following *Two Piece Combo to Achieve Financial Discipline.*

Two-Piece Combo to Achieve Financial Discipline.

1. **Set a yearly financial goal.** Set a yearly financial goal (i.e. $1,000 or $5,000 or $10,000, or $20,000, etc) that you can afford.

2. **Set a certain smaller amount aside**. Set a certain smaller amount aside each month towards achieving your financial goal (i.e. $100 or $500 or $1,000, or $2,000, etc). Please make sure that the amount you decide to put aside each month is something that you can afford.

By setting your yearly financial goal and making monthly strides to accomplish it, you are on your way to achieving financial discipline. Now use it to unlock more financial options for yourself and your family in your future (i.e. retirement when you decide; a nicer home for your family; college tuition and expenses; a nice family vacation).

On the following page is the *Investitude Financial Discipline* chart that will help you to set yearly financial goals and determine how much you will need to put aside each year in order to achieve your financial goals. In using this chart, pick an amount to consistently save each month and watch as it accumulates. Please use it as a tool to help you to plan and apply financial discipline to your life.

	M:	1	2	3	4	5	6	Total
LEV.	**AMT**	$	$	$	$	$	$	$
1	**100**	100	200	300	400	500	600	600
2	**200**	200	400	600	800	1000	1200	1200
3	**300**	300	600	900	1200	1500	1800	1800
4	**400**	400	800	1200	1600	2000	2400	2400
5	**500**	500	1000	1500	2000	2500	3000	3000
6	**600**	600	1200	1800	2400	3000	3600	3600
7	**700**	700	1400	2100	2800	3500	4200	4200
8	**800**	800	1600	2400	3200	4000	4800	4800
9	**900**	900	1800	2700	3600	4500	5400	5400
10	**1000**	1000	2000	3000	4000	5000	6000	6000
11	**1100**	1100	2200	3300	4400	5500	6600	6600
12	**1200**	1200	2400	3600	4800	6000	7200	7200
13	**1300**	1300	2600	3900	5200	6500	7800	7800
14	**1400**	1400	2800	4200	5600	7000	8400	8400
15	**1500**	1500	3000	4500	6000	7500	9000	9000
16	**1600**	1600	3200	4800	6400	8000	9600	9600
	M:	**1**	**2**	**3**	**4**	**5**	**6**	**Total**

	M:	7	8	9	10	11	12	Total
LEV.	**AMT**	$	$	$	$	$	$	$
1	**100**	700	800	900	1000	1100	1200	1200
2	**200**	1400	1600	1800	2000	2200	2400	2400
3	**300**	2100	2400	2700	3000	3300	3600	3600
4	**400**	2800	3200	3600	4000	4400	4800	4800
5	**500**	3500	4000	4500	5000	5500	6000	6000
6	**600**	4200	4800	5400	6000	6600	7200	7200
7	**700**	4900	5600	6300	7000	7700	8400	8400
8	**800**	5600	6400	7200	8000	8800	9600	9600
9	**900**	6300	7200	8100	9000	9900	10800	10800
10	**1000**	7000	8000	9000	10000	11000	12000	12000
11	**1100**	7700	8800	9900	11000	12100	13200	13200
12	**1200**	8400	9600	10800	12000	13200	14400	14400
13	**1300**	9100	10400	11700	13000	14300	15600	15600
14	**1400**	9800	11200	12600	14000	15400	16800	16800
15	**1500**	10500	12000	13500	15000	16500	18000	18000
16	**1600**	11200	12800	14400	16000	17600	19200	19200
	M:	**7**	**8**	**9**	**10**	**11**	**12**	**Total**

Financial Discipline Chart:

How much can you plan to put aside after the following years?

Year #1 __________

Year #2 __________

Year#3 __________

Year#4 __________

Year#5 __________

TOTAL: __________

(The total is reflective of the amount of money accumulated and/or saved after only 5 years of using the ***Investitude Financial Discipline Chart***.)

Lev=Level Amt=Amount M=Months

What if I get off track with my yearly financial goals?

If you get off track with achieving your yearly financial goals, don't worry or stress yourself out! Instead, it is more important to learn from it, pick yourself up, and continue to strive towards achieving as close to your financial goal as is feasibly possible for that particular year. Remember, saving something is better than saving nothing at all. Then, take a *time out* to reflect on *what happened* and/or what ultimately caused your financial goal to be derailed. Then, use that particular insight to readjust **not** the yearly financial goal but the amount put aside each month towards achieving your yearly financial goal. As my mother would say, "I would rather finish [the race] having something, instead of nothing."

3. Strategically Positioning Yourself

Strategically positioning yourself with your financial goals in mind means that you are working to accomplish a twofold plan: (1) earning money while also (2) aligning your work situation as a means to accomplish one of your financial goals. This can best be brought to light with the following examples:

I. The person that works at a mediocre job to earn enough to live and cover the closing costs on their new home for their family.

(Strategic Positioning: Purchasing a Home)

II. The person that works at a grocery store and is also using his/her wages to cover the cost of a college degree or technical training program.

(Strategic Positioning: Higher Education)

III. The college student that takes a flexible job because of management opportunities, a work-schedule that accommodates her class schedule, and the company offers a college tuition reimbursement plan.

(Strategic Positioning: Flexible Schedule, Management Opportunities, College Tuition Reimbursement Plan.)

IV. The person that took a temporary sales job or a job paying commission only in order to quickly earn the start-up capital to open up their own business.

Strategic Positioning: Opening up their own business.

V. The person that takes a job at a computer store and uses it to get a discount on a functional laptop.

Strategic Positioning: Laptop.

These are all examples of what it means to strategically position yourself with your financial goals in mind. By strategically positioning yourself, you are able to use the job to accomplish the extra!

Also, please note that the job is <u>not worth it</u> if it causes you to get caught up with unethical business practices that require you to compromise your body, integrity, beliefs, values, and/or who you are as a person! Alternatively, if it is illegal, it is also <u>not worth it</u>. Realize that there is no reason to get involved with unethical business enterprises or illegal activities for the sake of earning money. There are too many legitimate opportunities available just waiting to receive your job application.

By strategically aligning yourself with your financial goals in mind, it allows you to earn money while also providing a means to strategically accomplish more of your financial goals. For more creative means to strategically position yourself to achieve your financial goals, please see Unit III on X-Factors.

In all, these techniques will help you to better understand your residual income and use it to accomplish your financial goals. I pray that this insight from me has been able to be a blessing unto you.

A Conversation with the Author:

No More Living from Paycheck to Paycheck

Using less than $100 to accomplish your financial goals can be a lot of fun especially when it involves (1) planning and (2) applying those dollars to the *Investitude Financial Discipline Chart.* The *Investitude Financial Discipline Chart* is not only something that the Lord gave to me and blessed me to design, but also something that I often reference with my own personal finances. Moreover, it has served as a very useful tool in not only helping me to have financial discipline, but also in helping me to accomplish some of my personal aspirations that require huge financial commitments.

First, I used it to help me to figure out how much money I could reasonably put aside each year as a good-faith down payment towards my fiancé's (now wife) diamond ring. And if you have ever walked down that *isle,* you would know that those pretty little diamonds cost much more than *bright, shinny, pennies.* I also used this chart to juggle how much I could reasonably save each year while also managing real life bills such as a mortgage, electricity, insurance, and several others. It has helped my wife and I to reasonably save an amount each year to plan annual vacations to such places as: Italy (Rome and Florence) and London. It has also provided some excellent guidance when it has come to managing the load of paying for graduate school while also living real life. But, what most people do not know is that I have been able to achieve these financial aspirations by putting less than $100.00 aside each month. Yes, that's right, most of these personal aspirations or financial goals were achieved by putting less than $100.00 aside each month. Now, you can use it too!

Below, I included the Investitude Financial Discipline Chart for less than $100.00. I am confident that it will help you to juggle your finances and save a lot of money towards achieving some of your financial aspirations (i.e. traveling, wedding planning, college tuition, opening up a business, and more) for less than $100.00 put aside each month. I pray that this chapter of my life has been able to be a blessing unto yours.

Financial Discipline Chart (Version 2)

Achieving Financial Goals by Saving Less Than $100/month

	M:	1	2	3	4	5	6	Total
LEV.	**AMT**	$	$	$	$	$	$	$
1	**100**	100	200	300	400	500	600	600
2	**90**	90	180	270	360	450	540	540
3	**80**	80	160	240	320	400	480	480
4	**75**	75	150	225	300	375	450	450
5	**70**	70	140	210	280	350	420	420
6	**65**	65	130	195	260	325	390	390
7	**60**	60	120	180	240	300	360	360
8	**55**	55	110	165	220	275	330	330
9	**50**	50	100	150	200	250	300	300
10	**40**	40	80	120	160	200	240	240
11	**35**	35	70	105	140	175	210	210
12	**30**	30	60	90	120	150	180	180
13	**20**	20	40	60	80	100	120	120
14	**10**	10	20	30	40	50	60	60
15	**5**	5	10	15	20	25	30	30
16	**1**	2	2	3	4	5	6	6
	M:	**1**	**2**	**3**	**4**	**5**	**6**	**Total**

Financial Discipline Chart (Version 2)

Achieving Financial Goals by Saving Less Than $100/month

	M:	7	8	9	10	11	12	Total
LEV.	**AMT**	$	$	$	$	$	$	$
1	**100**	700	800	900	1000	1100	1200	1200
2	**90**	630	720	810	900	990	1080	1080
3	**80**	560	640	720	800	880	960	960
4	**75**	525	600	675	750	825	900	900
5	**70**	490	560	630	700	770	840	840
6	**65**	455	520	585	650	715	780	780
7	**60**	420	480	540	600	660	720	720
8	**55**	385	440	495	550	605	660	660
9	**50**	350	400	450	500	550	600	600
10	**40**	280	320	360	400	440	480	480
11	**35**	245	280	315	350	385	420	420
12	**30**	210	240	270	300	330	360	360
13	**20**	140	160	180	200	220	240	240
14	**10**	70	80	90	100	110	120	120
15	**5**	35	40	45	50	55	60	60
16	**1**	7	8	9	10	11	12	12
	M:	**7**	**8**	**9**	**10**	**11**	**12**	**Total**

Chapter V

Light Bulb Effect:
Turning On Your Residual Income

Light Bulb Effect: Turning <u>On</u> Your Residual Income

"Don't let what you can't do interfere with what you can do."

Anonymous

Most people *wish* that they made more money. Have you ever found yourself looking at your paycheck and saying, *"I wish I made just a little bit more?"* Or, maybe you have either heard yourself or someone else saying that other familiar frustrating phrase, *"I just don't make enough money..."* In either case, if you have ever heard these expressions or said them yourself, don't feel bad. The reality is that when most people are making these comments, they are actually speaking the truth—which is *they need and deserve to make more money!*

These statements are also very revealing. For some people, they could be indicative of their past experiences, their upbringing, or their earnings before they were struck by some unexpected tragedy (i.e. bankruptcy, divorce, a sudden illness or death, job layoffs, etc). All in all, these comments tell us a lot about the subjective beliefs and/or background of the speaker and that they likely have a myriad of reasons to justify their feelings. The bottom line is that the people making these comments do **not** believe that their job or career is paying them enough to financially sustain them and allow them to move up in life. But, there's a solution! And it doesn't involve getting a new job, a second job, working overtime, or donating your organs for money. Instead, it involves paying attention to your driving habits. Allow me to explain.

How do you drive?

Some people handle their money the way they drive a car to get home after a busy day at work (or school). Imagine this: You are stalled in rush hour traffic at a busy intersection and the only thing you can *see* holding up traffic in front of you is a huge, heavy-duty, freight truck. As the driver of a smaller economy-sized car, you are also aware that you are handicapped by the trucks' immense size and slow pace as you are unable to see around it as it moves as slow as a snail. You begin to impatiently look in the other lanes as you can see and hear other vehicles quickly *zooming, rooming,* and *beep-beeping* on by you. So you prepare to do the dangerous and unthinkable. You signal and speed out in one of the other lanes in hopes of *zooming, rooming, and beep-beeping* in front of that BIG TRUCK.

However, at your first opportunity, and without even really considering consequences, you risk your life by quickly leaping OUT and into a fast-moving lane to get around the huge, heavy-duty freight truck. Other cars are quickly on your tail. Someone swerves to avoid hitting you; someone else madly starts to honk as if an alarm has been sounded because the car that swerved away from hitting you has almost hit them; a person driving a pick-up truck gives you a cold, guilty stare in acknowledgement of the wrong you have just done; and many of the drivers of the cars in the farthest lane away from you are all looking at you and shaking their heads in discontentment with your action. But you did it! You finally got around that BIG, SLOW, huge, heavy-duty, freight truck only to see something that you didn't expect. That's when you realize that it was not the truck slowing up traffic (or how much money you make), but it's the one smaller car that you couldn't see in front of the truck that was stalling traffic. And now, you are being detained again because there are other cars in front of you.

A small obstacle like a slow moving truck stopped by a smaller vehicle in front of it could have caused you to lose your life or cause someone else to lose his or hers by getting into a horrible accident. Or, cause you to injure someone else due to road rage. All of these negative externalities could have occurred all based upon a misconception. But, the real problem was not the truck that was stalling your financial traffic, but what was in front of the truck that is blocking your financial traffic.

The reality is that most people handle their finances in this way. They see that big truck in front of them and start getting frustrated and saying "I don't make enough money!" as the reason why their financial traffic is blocked. They respond by eagerly attempting to jump in front of that truck by blaming their financial woes on not making enough. They respond by working more jobs for more hours. But in the end, they still end up losing because they spend less time with family and friends, risking their life and the lives of their family, suffer from stress and other types of illnesses created through stress, suffer from mental break downs, losing a marriage, missing their children's performances (e.g., baseball, football, basketball, cheerleading, dance) and others. All in all, they risk and lose so much just to earn that *additional dollar* just to realize that it really wasn't worth it in the first place because they are still in the same financial debacle or worst, then before.

Consequently, they risked their life just to come to the conclusion that there is still something blocking their financial traffic and it's not just that truck. So please allow me to provide you with some solutions to help you identify the *license plate* of the real problem that could be slowing down your financial traffic and help you to find more money from what you already have.

Solution #1: Create a Budget.

Budgeting is easy! All you do is just plug in the numbers in the **Investitude Budgeting**

Worksheet below. Please note that the column listed as "Category" identifies the potential names of both **revenues** and **expenses**. Revenues serve as valuable income that you receive. Expenses are the bills and other forms of things that you have to spend towards. The next column is noted as "Monthly Revenues" or "Monthly Expenses." This is where you actually include the total monthly amount for the various categories. The second column is called the "Monthly Goal." It is the column that you should use in order to set your financial goals in terms of how much you actually would like to earn and/or reduce your expenses by each month. Lastly, the expense column listed as "Difference" is how much you would like to save between what you pay now and your anticipated expense goal. The *Investitude Budgeting Worksheet* should help you to accurately pinpoint what financial resources you have to work with. If you have money left over (more revenues than expenses), you are considered in the **black**, which is technically in a healthy financial position. But, if you have more expenses than you have money, you are considered in the **red**, which could technically be a very dangerous financial place to live. Please complete the *Investitude Budgeting Worksheet* below and remember, rule #2: You can write in me!

Note: For revenues and expenses incurred more frequently (e.g., gas) or less frequently (e.g., auto insurance), convert the payment to a monthly amount when calculating the monthly budget.

Investitude Budget For:

______________________________ on ______

(name) (Date)

Category	Monthly Revenue	Monthly Income Earning Goal	
Residual Income			
Wages			
Bonuses			
Investment Income			
Interest Income			
Other Income:			
Other Income:			
Other Income:			
Other Income:			
Residual Income Total	A:		

Category	Monthly Expense	Monthly Expense Goal (How much can you reduce this expense by?)	Difference (Monthly Expense – Monthly Goal)
Expenses			
Tithes/ Gifts / Donations			
Home Expenses:			
Mortgage or Rent			
Home Insurance			
Property Taxes			
Home Repairs/Maintenance/ etc.			
Utilities:			
Electricity			
Water and Sewer			
Natural Gas or Oil			
Food:			
Groceries			
Eating Out, Lunches, Snacks			

Misc. Food Expenses:			
Family Obligations			
Day Care, Babysitting			
Child Support			
Health and Medical			
Insurance (medical, dental, vision)			
Doctor Visit Fee			
Fitness (Gym, Massage, Spa, Vitamins.)			
Transportation			
Car Payments			
Gasoline/Oil			
Auto Repairs/Maintenance/Fees			
Auto Insurance			
Other Transportation (tolls, bus, subway, taxis)			
Debt Payments			
Credit Cards			
Student Loans			
Other Loans			
Leisure Time			
Cable or Satellite TV			
Shopping			
Hobbies			
Subscriptions and Dues			
Vacations			
Pets			
Food			
Vet. Fees			
Miscellaneous			
Grooming			
Pampering			
Business Related Expenses			

Computer Expense			
Wireless Internet (or other internet related charges)			
Business Incorporation			
Office Lease			
Investments and Savings:			
High-Yielding Saving Account			
Bonds			
Stocks or /Mutual Funds			
College Fund			
Savings (bank, credit union, etc.)			
Emergency Fund			
IRAs			
401K (or other similar plan)			
Total Expenses & Investments/Savings	B:		
Surplus or Shortage (Income minus total expenses and investments)	Surplus Of:		Shortage Of:
A – B =			
	BLACK		**RED**

Remember, if you have money left over (more revenues "A" than expenses "B"), you are considered in the **black**, which is technically in a healthy financial position. But, if you have more expenses "B" than you have income "A", you are considered in the **red**, which could technically be a very dangerous financial place to live.

* * *

AFTERMATH:

Were you in the Black?
Or
Were you in the Red?

Now that we have laid everything down on the table, let's go to your financial position and work to specifically address your financial needs. If you were in the Red, please visit Chapter 6. Alternatively, if you were in the black, please visit Chapter 7. These chapters will provide assistance in specifically addressing your financial needs in aiding to turn on the light of your residual income. Before leaving, please be sure to revisit the *Investitude Budget Worksheet* to make sure that the next chapter you read is the right Investitude for you! I pray that this chapter from me has been able to be a blessing unto you.

If red, go to Chapter 6. If black, go to Chapter 7.

A Conversation with the Author:

Reflection on Second Chances

Don't blame yourself if your finances are not in order! Just take some time to work at it to get it where you want it to be. What you were doing before made perfect sense – that was all you knew. But now, you have a solution; and with that solution there is a second chance (or a third, fourth, seventeenth, or however many chances you need) to get it right! It makes perfect sense why most people blame financial woes and problems on things that are not truly affecting their finances like trucks. This confirms that one of the most challenging tasks for some people is to stop passing the blame for their problems and figure out what's really affecting them.

From my experience, what has proved helpful is to first pray and then jot down every expense and revenue. Afterward, plug in the numbers on a chart (or paper) and analyze your spending habits until they make sense. Sometimes, this would help me to understand why I had so much money left to save and invest while other times it revealed the naked, grim truth that I had overspent my means for the month. While budgeting is definitely not one of most people's favorite pastimes, I pray that it will become something that you enjoy doing. Hopefully, this daily routine will help you to become a better steward of your finances and help you to turn on the light of your residual income. Keep marching onward and upwards to reaching your financial goals. I pray that you continue to enjoy the *Investitude Budgeting Worksheet* and that this chapter of my life has been a blessing unto yours.

Chapter VI

Residual Income: Red Zone

Residual Income: RED Zone

"Failure is not the worst thing in the world. The very worst is not to try."

Anonymous

Welcome to the Red Zone! It doesn't matter how you got here, my top priority is to help you to get out. But in order for us to be successful, I will need a threefold commitment: First, I need you to have a positive attitude! Secondly, I will need you not to damper that positive attitude by worrying about your finances. If you fail to commit to this suggestion, unfortunately, you may always be in the red. The reason that worrying is so dangerous is because worrying doesn't change anything; but it could create unexpected health problems such as those associated with stress, anxiety, and others. It can also tear a person or family apart. So please, don't stress and enjoy the process of getting out of the Red.

Mathew 6:27, teaches an important lesson about worrying. It says, "Who of you by worrying can add a single hour to his [or her] life?" This profound question reminds us that worrying won't ever change a thing. So instead of worrying, relax and try to reflect on the things that you have. Also, look at brighter side of things by acknowledging *that things could always be much worse* and that at least you have taken a proactive role in improving your finances by reading through this chapter.

Lastly, I need you to concern yourself with your finances. This means be willing to either put in the time or make the time to apply the principals learned in this chapter and throughout this book to get out of the red. I'm not asking you to think that making time and doing these suggestions will change your finances overnight, but I am asking that you at least make a good-faith effort to try your best to apply the lessons learned to your life. In concerning yourself with your finances, I am also asking you to be a cooperative reader. This means I need you to actually act on the suggestions and information that you have been given.

So let's stay calm as we work together to boost your financial position. Here are 21 tips to get you out of the red. If correctly implemented, I am confident that you will be glad that you temporarily stopped by to visit this chapter.

21 Tips to get you out of the Red

1. Modify Your Expenses.

First, revisit your *Investitude Budget*. Try using the monthly goal column to set a goal at reducing certain bills. An example of this could be the following:

Cell Phone Bill - $55 per month.
Goal: Reduce bill by $10 per month.
Modification: remove text-messaging features and stop using 411 services to reduce monthly bill by $10.

2. Slash Expenses

Then, if modifying your expenses is not helpful, try to remove things completely from your budget that you don't need. To make this process as easy as possible, use a red pin and simply slash through the items on your budget that you could go without. Some of the more obvious ones may include: entertainment expenses, eating out at restaurants, etc. Or, alternatively slashing a monthly cell phone bill and moving to a prepaid phone that offers free nights and/or weekends may be a feasible solution for you that will save you money as well.

3. Reduce your biggest expenses.

Go to the largest expenses (i.e. mortgage or rent payments, college expenses, car payments, utilities, and insurance) blocking your financial traffic and find out if you could have any of these items reduced. This task can usually be accomplished by contacting the company that the expense is being paid towards and finding out if that particular company has any programs that may be able to help you.

Some of these companies may offer programs that (1) help reduce your payments, (2) provide you with more flexibility, and/or (3) refer you to an agency or faith-based organization that can temporarily make a one-time benevolent payment towards your bill(s) to help you out.

4. Make Sure What You Pay Is Accurate!

Companies, machines, credit cards, and human beings share the commonality that they are all prone to error. As a result, some of your expenses in the form of bills, fees, etc. could be incorrect. In order to cure this problem, simply review your statements (and/or expenses) and contact the company with your findings and/or questions to make sure that what you are paying is the correct amount. If you find out that you have been paying a much higher amount than what you were supposed to, be sure to ask for the prorated amount (which means that you are asking to be compensated for any overage that was paid towards the expense). By making sure you are paying the correct amounts, it will help you to save more in the long run.

5. Home Owners: Removing PMI.

If you have a home mortgage, try removing private mortgage insurance (PMI). PMI is an unnecessary expense that mortgage companies factor into the amount of your mortgage until you reach a minimum payment amount. However, most mortgage companies will not automatically remove PMI (irregardless of you meeting the minimum amount) unless you instruct them to do so.

In order to have PMI removed, simply contact the mortgage company and have them to review your payment history to find out if you have met the minimum requirements to have PMI removed. This easy process (that may take you less than 5 minutes to do) can easily save you thousands of dollars in your pocket that you may have unnecessarily been paying to your mortgage company. For more information on PMI, please read Unit V on Investing.

6. Insurance: Inquire About Discounts.

Try contacting your insurance company (i.e. auto, health, etc.) to find out if they offer any discounts. Some of these discounts may include specials for: senior citizens, volunteers, students, students that make good grades, and others. It is also a good practice to inquire about other special discounts that the insurance company may offer which will save you money in helping to reduce your monthly premium.

7. Mortgage: Discounts for Timely Payment.

Contact your mortgage company to find out if there are discounts for making your payment at certain times in the month (i.e., $1,000 monthly insurance that is due on the 15th may actually be only $985.00 if paid on the first of the month).

8. Electric Bill: Check for Plans

The electricity company may have an energy reduction plan that they can tell you about that may help to free up more money in your budget. Alternatively, the electric company can usually send out someone at no charge to read your electrical meter to determine if it has any errors. If it does have errors, a correction to this problem will obviously fix your electrical bill especially when you ask for the prorated amount to be reflective of the length of time that the problem existed. Also, please note that new homes and older homes could both have problems with their electrical meters. Therefore, it's a good practice to have your meters checked for errors.

9. Check Statements Regularly for Identity Theft

This occurrence is all too common in today's society. Request hard copies of your monthly statements to be mailed to you and check them regularly for withdrawals that did not come from you or an authorized user. Reporting identity theft will result in an investigation and if the allegations prove true, most companies will reimburse your account the fraudulently procured amounts.

10. Review Payment Plans.

Don't just blindly pay bills because you receive them in the mail. Request itemized statements of the charges and double check to make sure that you are not paying for something that is already paid off. In today's automated society, accounts get mixed up and you might accidentally be charged for someone else's debt. Make sure that you are paying what rightfully belongs to you.

11. Use Coupons for Shopping

Coupons can save you tons of money and they are easy to get. All you do is check the newspaper for companies to go grocery shopping. In addition, change up your shopping habits and plan to purchase items from discount stores. Often, you can find almost identical generic items or heavily discounted name brand items from lesser-known discount stores (i.e., Big Lots, Dollar Stores, and others). Also, don't make impulse purchases at the store but shop with a planned shopping list and stick to it!

12. Buy Items at a Discount

Many new items depreciate the moment you leave the store with them. Shop online at Ebay (www.Ebay.com) or Craigslist (www.Craigslist.org). These venues allow you to buy brand new items or items that have been used modestly at a discount. The technology is simple and it is worth learning to take advantage of the tremendous discounts.

13. Turn off or Reduce the Cell Phone!

This can be temporarily (until you are in a position to increase your finances) or permanently. Shop around to find plans that are competitive and offer *only the features that you need.* Avoid extra features that add on to your monthly charge (i.e., text messaging, internet, dialing 411, custom ring tones, etc.) and stick to the basic services.

14. Consider alternative means of transportation

With the increasing cost of gas, it may be a good idea to consider carpooling with your relatives or neighbors that you trust that are headed to similar destinations. Also, for families, plan your trips before you take them so that you can maximize your gas by picking certain days to travel and run all of your errands in that area on those particular days. Also, consider public transportation (i.e., a bus system, metro or subway) as an affordable alternative.

15. Write out a Payment Plan

If you owe money to a hospital or some other type of public entity, it may be in your best interest to work out a payment plan. Simply contact the company and speak to them about creating a payment plan. For example, if you have a $3,000 medical bill, you could agree to pay them $30.00 per month. Although you will be paying this for a while, this type of agreement may stop the company from sending the bill to a collection company and adding it to your credit report while also allowing you the time to manage the debt. Remember, your goal is **not to pay all of your bills and have nothing left over**. Instead, you want to create a plan that allows you to pay amounts gradually to debtors (especially those that do not have revolving interest rates) while freeing up funds that you can save and invest wisely to plan for your financial future.

16. Create a Receipt Wall

On this wall, you attach all your weekly bills and receipts to find out where your money is going. You will be amazed by all of the things that your money goes toward but you never even realized it because it was not on the radar.

17. Buy used cars

New cars **depreciate** (lose value) the moment you drive them off of the car dealership lot. Learn to research deals and buy used cars in good condition that you can purchase with cash or pay off quickly. Not having a monthly car note will free up a substantial amount of funds each month that you can use toward saving, investing and implementing your financial plan.

Consider buying vehicles from family members, estate sales, from rental car companies or repossession sales as long as the car has value and they are selling it for a deal. Always have them inspected by a mechanic you trust so that you can properly assess the value and costs of any repairs needed. Before you purchase them, confirm their value by referencing the Kelly Blue Book (available in bookstores and libraries).

18. Eliminate Credit Card Debts

You will be amazed at how much of your monthly income you will be able to keep in your pocket if you eliminate credit card debt and only purchase what you can pay for with cash. The interest rates on credit continually consume your money especially if you are only making the minimum payments. Aggressively paying off the cards will give you freedom and free up your funds to do other things.

19. Don't keep excess cash in your pocket.

The more you have in your pocket or purse, the more likely you will spend that day. Therefore, put your money in a less conspicuous place than your pocket or purse and save yourself from spending. A good place to hide your excess money is in your bank account.

20. Reduce your Cable or Satellite Bill

Companies win by selling you expensive packages with tons of features that make you think you're getting a bargain. Instead, reduce your cable bill and similar products to the basic package that consists of the functions you need. You don't really watch all of the channels that you have. Many television shows are for free on their network's websites or available for purchase as a collection on DVD. You can also read the information from verbal newscasts by using the free Internet at a public library or college campus. Additionally, special shows are often featured on YouTube.com or you can always meet at a friend's house to watch them. Alternatively, you can have cable or satellite completely removed.

21. Reduce monthly subscriptions

Most public libraries subscribe to almost every magazine and keep copies within their collections. Make a regular visit to the library to read your favorite publications as opposed to subscribing to them all. Many libraries now allow you to check out CDs and DVDs of popular movies in addition to just books. Therefore, you can reduce your monthly spending budget on these items by utilizing the free services.

After implementing these 21 solutions to your life, try to budget your finances again and see what comes up. If this insight has not got you out of the red, then remember that you are a work in progress and as such you are still on your way. As you may be metaphorically about to turn the page to exit the Red Zone, you may also be close to exiting the red in your life by making the time, implementing these strategies, and being concerned about your finances.

Congratulations in advance on journeying this far as your time in the red is about to end. I pray that this chapter from me has been able to be a blessing unto you.

A Conversation with the Author:
Strategically Aligning Your Bill Payments

Sometimes it's not that you don't make enough to pay your bills, but the bills are hitting you at the wrong time. Sometimes, bills are scheduled to be due at a time when you don't have any money (or not enough). Or, since you have so many bills at the same time that you can't pay them all. If this is your problem, you should try to align your bill payments to when you have the cash to pay them. If you doubt that you can do this, I won't you to know that as a rule of thumb: Companies want to get paid! Because of this, most companies will allow their clients to adjust their bill payments to when it is convenient for the bill payer (you). In other words, if all your bills hit between the 1st and the 5th, some companies will allow you to spread your bill due dates where as two bills may hit between the 1st and the 5th while the others hit between the 15th through the 20th. In order to adjust your bill due date(s), all you do is the following:

1. Contact the company

2. Ask to speak to a customer service representative and be sure to document all of their information in your business journal (their full name, employer identification number, the date and time of the

conversation, and the name of their manager and/or supervisor) for future reference.

3. Tell the customer service representative that "I would like to adjust the due date on my bill from _______ to sometime around the ______."

   (Please be sure to review your calendar to make sure that the dates you added in the blanks above will work for your personal payment schedule.)

4. The customer service representative will likely respond by asking you something similar to "When can you afford to pay it?" At this point, the ball is in your court to determine the time during the month that is most convenient for you to pay your bill. However, if the customer service representative says that it cannot be changed, this may indicate that it is not that particular company's policy to change your payment date.

5. Also ask if there are any charges for the adjustment and how the adjustment will affect your bill(s).

Strategically aligning your bills can come in handy anytime that you are trying to adjust your bills to fit your specific needs. I pray that this chapter from me has been able to be a blessing unto you.

Chapter VII

Residual Income: BLACK

Residual Income: Black

*"**In the black,** operating at a profit or being out of debt (opposed to in the red)."*

Popular Idioms

Welcome to the Black! I'm glad that you are here. My goal in this chapter is to help you to save even more money, which will further increase your power of choices and overall financial health. Here are some tips to help you to be successful at doing so.

9 Helpful Hints to Help You to Save

1. Review Payment Plans.

Don't just blindly pay bills because you receive them in the mail. Request itemized statements of the charges and double check to make sure that you are not paying for something that is already paid off. In today's automated society, accounts get mixed up and you might accidentally be charged for someone else's debt. Make sure that you are paying what rightfully belongs to you.

2. Use Coupons for Shopping

Coupons can save you tons of money and they are easy to get. All you do is check the newspaper for companies to go grocery shopping. In addition, change up your shopping habits and plan to purchase items from discount stores. Often, you can find almost identical generic items or heavily discounted name brand items from lesser-known discount stores (i.e., Big Lots, Dollar Stores, etc.). Also, don't make impulse purchases at the store but shop with a planned shopping list and stick to it!

3. Buy Items at a Discount

Many new items depreciate the moment you leave the store with them. Shop online at Ebay (www.Ebay.com) or Craigslist (www.Craigslist.org). These venues allow you to buy brand new items or items that have been used modestly at a discount. The technology is simple and it is worth learning to take advantage of the tremendous discounts.

4. Create a Receipt Wall

On this wall, you attach all your weekly bills and receipts to find out where your money is going. You will be amazed by all of the things and places that your money goes toward but you never even realize because it was not on the radar.

5. Buy used cars

New cars **depreciate** (lose value) the moment you drive them off of the car dealership lot. Learn to research deals and buy used cars in good condition that you can purchase with cash or pay off quickly. Not having a monthly car note will free up a substantial amount of funds each month that you can use toward saving, investing and implementing your financial plan. Consider buying vehicles from family members, estate sales, from rental car companies or repossession sales as long as the car has value and they are selling it for a deal. Always have them inspected by a mechanic you trust so that you can properly assess the value and costs of any repairs needed. Before you purchase them, confirm their value by referencing the Kelly Blue Book (available in bookstores and libraries).

6. Eliminate Credit Card Debts

You will be amazed at how much of your monthly income you will be able to keep in your pocket if you eliminate credit card debt(s) and only purchase what you can pay for with cash. The interest rates on credit continually consume your money especially if you are only making the minimum payments. Aggressively paying off the cards will give you freedom and free up your funds to do other things.

7. Don't keep excess cash in your pocket

The more you have in your pocket or purse, the more likely you will spend it that day. Therefore, put your money in a less conspicuous place than your pocket or purse and save yourself from spending. A good place to keep your excess money is in your bank account.

8. Reduce your Cable or Satellite Bill

Companies win by selling you expensive packages with tons of features that make you think you're getting a bargain. Instead, reduce your cable bill and similar products to the basic package that consists of the functions you need. You don't really watch all of the channels that you have. Many television shows are for free on their network's websites or available for purchase as a collection on DVD. You can also read the information from verbal newscasts by using the free internet at a public library or college campus. Additionally, special shows are often featured on YouTube.com or you can always meet at a friend's house to watch them. Alternatively, you can have cable or satellite completely removed to save even more.

9. Reduce monthly subscriptions

Most public libraries subscribe to almost every magazine and keep copies within their collections. Make a regular visit to the library to read your favorite publications as opposed to subscribing to them all. Many libraries now allow you to check out CDs and DVDs of popular movies in addition to just books. Therefore, you can reduce your monthly spending budget on these items by utilizing the free services.

A Conversation with the Author:

Having a Credit Card Exit Plan

Determining which credit card to pay off first is difficult to answer because there are so many personal variables to consider. Therefore, sharing a general rule is not fair because it may help some, but hurt others. So, what I will share is what I do prior to signing up for a credit card—*I write out a **Credit Card Exit Plan**.*

As I've already mentioned, when I planned to purchase my wife her diamond ring, it was not a cheap endeavor. In fact, I had to honestly resort to putting that piece of jewelry on a one-year layaway plan and then after that time had expired (and the people called me demanding I pick it up), I purchased the difference on the jewelry company's credit card. But, I wasn't even close to being free and clear as I had thousands of dollars in diamond debt now looming over my head. To make matters worse, the card also had a 47% interest rate that was guaranteed to also hit me in the face within six months if I had not paid the diamond off within that time frame. In addition, there was a clause that I read in the card agreement (and please always read the card agreement) that said something to the effect that if I were to ever miss a payment for whatever reason, the company would be able to tack on the 47% interest immediately and the six month grace period would permanently be waived. I was in a grim situation with a mortgage and several other bills to also pay. But, there was good news in the fact that I had already planned for this occasion by making a Credit Card Exit Plan.

The first thing I did was pray and asked God to comfort me and allow me to stick to the **exit plan**. Next, I revisited the exit plan by looking over how much money I had figured prior to signing up for the credit card, I would have to put toward this plan in order to effectively exit this credit card without reaping a negative outcome. Then I applied it! Here are the details.

I took the total amount left to pay on the diamond and divided it by six (six represented the combined total number of months and grace period that I had to completely pay off the diamond in order to avoid penalty). Then, I cut out and reduced certain expenses (i.e. entertainment and shopping expenses as well as my cell phone bill was also reduced). Other personal expenses were also reduced. At the same time while all of this was going on, as referenced in my exit plan, I used some of the money that I had put aside from using the *Investitude Discipline Chart* towards making monthly diamond payments that were quadruple the meager amounts that the financial company was billing me for each month. Of course, it makes sense why the financial company was charging me such meager amounts as the financial company would profit tremendously if I didn't pay off the credit card in time as the company would be free to charge me more interest and fees for failure to pay off the full amount in the short-time period. Fortunately, within six months, I had completely paid off that diamond ring and called to close the account immediately.

I share this to say that just because you are in the *black* does not make you impervious to harm when it comes to dealing with credit cards, credit companies, or debts. Continue to be careful! One bad financial decision like not having an exit plan is all that it can take to really harm you and turn your financial health into financial sickness. Am I suggesting that you should not buy diamond rings or other expensive items? "No!" However, what I am suggesting is that if you consider credit cards and/or making expensive purchases, be mindful of the consequences that could ensue and more importantly, always have an exit plan prior to signing up for it. I pray that this chapter of my life has been able to be a blessing unto yours.

Chapter VIII

Clash of the Titans

Clash of the Titans

"Can two walk together except unless they agree?"
Amos 3:3 (King James Version)

A true clash of the Titans in any home, marriage, family, or business can come when there are two or more parties that fail to agree about their finances. These types of disagreements involving finances could range from issues such as creating a solid financial plan; deciding on financial goals; agreeing on retirement; determining where to put financial resources and others. One party might want to put the finances towards immediate bills while another may strive to put financial resources toward either saving and/or investing for the future. These are just some of the multitude of issues that may be in dispute. However, please be careful when broaching financial issues. These types of conflicts have the potential to become very ugly and have the potential to ruin homes, marriages, families, and/or businesses. At best, these disputes may transform into pointless quarrels that have nothing to do with finances.

Nevertheless, there is a solution for this clashing that can be accomplished in 10 easy steps. It will take the cooperation of **both** parties working together as a team to accomplish common goals. If you are ready to stop the clashing, here's how to find financial success as a team.

10 Solutions to End Financial Clashing

1. Agree to discuss your finances.

Pick an afternoon when all parties are free. Turn off your phones and other interruptions and select a quiet and confidential environment (e.g., your home living room) since you will be discussing very private matters.

2. Set Ground Rules.

These are the rules that you will use to discuss your finances. It's important that you both agree not to throw one another's short falls or mistakes at each other. However, you may address a particular situation in a neutral manner as long as you are not making it about the other person or using it for personal attack. Also, you must agree to not use curse words, name calling, or other derogatory language towards one another through the course of your discussion. Lastly, you must all agree that if one party does not agree with the other party, they are still okay.

3. Find Out the Concerns of Both Parties.

Give a sheet of paper to each person present. Have each side draft all their concerns on one side of the paper.

4. Find Out the Goals of Both Parties.

Then, without seeing the other person's concerns, on the back of the same paper, individually list your goals for the family, marriage, home, or business that you would like to see accomplished in the order of priority within the following time frames:

<u>Short-Term Goals</u>
Short-Term goals are goals that you would like to accomplish within a year up to five years. For example, fixing the plumbing; planning a summer vacation; paying for your semester of college; saving 40% of your income; buying a summer home or timeshare; and others.

<u>Long Term Goals</u>
Long-Term goals are goals that you would like to see accomplished over the next five to ten plus years. For example, retiring at the age of 35; eliminating your credit card debts and student loans; paying off your home mortgage; and others.

5. Share your individual concerns and goals with the other person.

Compare your list of goals with the other person. Listen intently to each other without interrupting. Ask questions (without attacking) in order to get a better understanding of the significance of the items listed

6. Determine your common goals.

Take your time and review the short term and long term goals that each of you articulated. Determine a final set of common goals that you can both agree on working towards.

7. List All of Your Joint Sources of Income and Joint Expenses.

Use the *Investitude Budget Worksheet* and include the combined incomes and expenses of both parties on an annual basis. Be sure to be honest and put all of your cards on the table.

8. Write a monthly budget.

This budget will become the plan of action to help you achieve your goals. Make sure you factor in undesignated funds for emergencies. Talk about the challenges that you both face and ways that you can keep each other accountable.

9. Follow-up.

Schedule a follow up meeting to revisit the plan at the end of each month to find out how well you were able to stick with it and determine ways to improve for the next month.

10. Celebrate your accomplishments!

Determine low budget ways of celebrating every time you fulfill a goal or achieve a landmark. For example, maybe celebrate with a movie night at home; or an affordable meal at your favorite restaurant; or a day trip to the beach each time you reach one of your goals.

I pray that the clashing in your home, family, marriage, or business cease to exist and that this chapter of my life has been able to be a blessing unto yours.

A Conversation with the Author:

Million Dollar Question

Okay, before I ask you the *Million Dollar Question,* I must forewarn you to not attempt to hide your answer by becoming defensive, pensive, or embarrassed. This question is one of the most challenging questions for most people to answer. When used in the wrong context, it can cause strong, successful, and confident individuals to feel embarrassed, and ashamed. It's the one question that etiquette books would forbid you to ask. We all try to hide it, yet we all know very well of its inevitable significance. So, through the context of Investitude, I humbly and respectfully ask you the million-dollar question, "How much do you make?"

"How much do you make?" Are you still wondering if I asked you what you think you just read, the answer is "Yes!" So let's be truthful and come clean by putting it all down on the table.

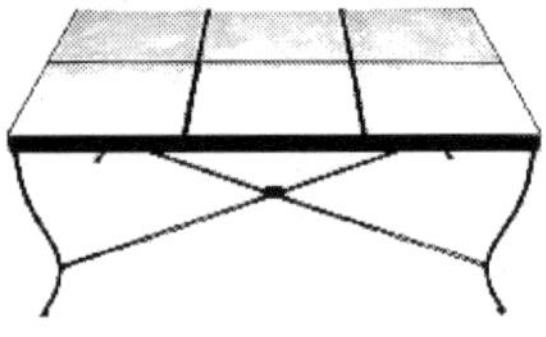

(Please place the amount on the table, not under the table.)

If you can be honest with me, about how much you make, you can also be honest with your spouse. Discussing money with a spouse could be one of the best decisions that you could ever make. My wife and I discuss our financial successes and failures all the time and I believe that this practice has been very good for our marriage. It also lets us know how to care for one another by financially addressing each other's needs. In addition, it helps us to share and selfless with one another instead of being selfish. I honestly believe that this type of open dialogue between us helps our marriage. I also believe that if more people started to discuss finances with spouses, there would be less people with divorces and less people feeling frustrated as if they are on their own when it comes to their finances.

In sharing this, please don't feel forced or obligated to do anything. All I want you to know is that honest disclosure and discourse with my spouse about our finances keeps us both smiling. I pray that this chapter of my life has been able to be a blessing unto yours.

Chapter IX

Full-Time Health Benefits on a Part-Time Work Schedule

Full-Time Health Benefits On a Part-Time Work Schedule

"The cards you hold in the game of life mean very little- it's the way you play them that counts."

Anonymous

Did you know that there are health and medical benefits available for part-time employees? Well, that's great news to know especially since one of the main reasons that cause uninsured people to experience financial setbacks is the out of pocket expenses associated with unexpected health and medical challenges. Unfortunately, any unexpected health challenge could be very expensive—easily costing you from thousands to ten thousands of dollars per emergency visit. But, there's good news. One, having health insurance could easily reduce the cost associated with unexpected health challenges tremendously. Two, this chapter will show you how to get health insurance for yourself, your family, or business on a part-time work schedule.

Moreover, the readers that will benefit most from this chapter are those who are interested in finding health benefits on a part-time schedule. Alternatively, anyone that is or would like to eventually become self-employed (a small business owner or start-up company owner) that cannot afford the cost of medical insurance will also benefit from this chapter. Entrepreneurial-minded readers that are contemplating stepping out of their comfort zone to open up their own business, but are only holding on to their current jobs due to medical coverage will also learn solutions to their dilemma. Furthermore, if you are the type of person that is willing to work for someone else—temporarily and on a part-time basis—in order to get your financial situation together as it relates to health benefits, then this insight will be invaluable for you. So let's cut across the field and move you closer toward scoring a healthy touchdown on a part-time basis.

How can I find Health Insurance on a Part-Time Schedule?

The following 3 easy ways can be used to find health benefits on a part-time work schedule:

1. Google this phrase: ***"Part-time jobs that offer benefits"***

Visit the website www.Google.com and search for the phrase listed above. Searching for the phrase on Google will yield numerous websites of part-time jobs that offer benefits. Of course, the drawback in using this method is that you will need time to sort through the material and try to reformat your Google phrase to be specific enough to address your area.

2. Try applying for part-time jobs in the following fields and services.

The following fields and services may offer part-time employees benefits: medical, government, and educational fields, as well as bus drivers, bartending, and postal services. In addition, some of the major bookstore and retail store chains may offer part-time benefits to its employees. Please contact specific companies that you may be interested in working for in the aforementioned areas and ask them if they offer benefits to part-time employees.

3. Try applying for jobs at these specific companies.

For a list of specific companies that offer benefits to their employees on a part-time basis, please visit: www.Investitude.com. If you also know of other companies that offer health or medical benefits on a part-time basis and would like to share it, please visit our website and we will share your insight and (if you allow us) acknowledge you for the information that you provided. Please visit www.Investitude.com for more information.

Are there other ways that I can get health insurance?

Yes, you can also get health insurance by purchasing it. If you would like to purchase health insurance, try *Googling* the following phrases: *"Online*

Health Insurance Quotes" and *"Online Health Insurance Coverage."*

This could serve as a resource in helping you to price affordable health insurance to meet all your personal, business, and/or other important needs. In addition, contacting the health insurance companies directly to find out if they have health benefit packets available for individuals, small businesses, or others for you to purchase can also be helpful.

I pray that this insight from me has been able to be a blessing unto you.

A Conversation with the Author:
Making the Sacrifice

Sometimes, in order to hold on to the right move and ultimately end up where we would like to be, it's important that we learn to put our ego aside and sacrifice toward the end goal. In doing so, I believe that working a part-time job for health and medical benefits and/or making other strategic alliances instead of working in order to *just* earn money are very clever, and savvy ways of achieving personal dreams, goals, and other aspirations for ourselves and/or family. But, sacrificing is not always easy, especially when you know that there is a CEO inside of you or a superb business idea waiting to be birthed here on earth. Some of your friends, family members, colleagues, associates, and others may even argue that the strength and patience that it will take is beyond you and/or if you don't step out right now, you are nothing but a weakling. But I disagree with this. In Ecclesiastes 3:1-10 (NIV), the Bible reminds us that there is a time and a season for everything, and if we can learn to trust God by waiting on His time and not our own, everything that you do will be right. Meaning, when you do finally step out with God's approval, your actions will be blessed. Am I suggesting that you become idle or push your idea aside? No! But, what I am suggesting is that before you step out, you use your time to build, develop, and expand your idea by first seeking God. And when the time comes, and He has approved it, let the world quake from the waves of success that will come from you. Once you do get to your place of promise and success, it won't really matter how many rude customers you encountered. Or, what people thought about you. Or what your critics had to say about you. The only thing that will matter is that you accomplished your goal and you did it, the right way, God's way. For that, there's an even bigger reward waiting for you. I pray that this insight from me has been able to be a blessing unto you.

Chapter X

Allowance

Allowance

"Train a child in the way he should go, and when he is old he will not turn from it."
Proverbs 22:6

If you are a parent, guardian or caretaker of a family, please read this chapter. This will allow you to understand the advantages of giving children an allowance, which is oftentimes perceived as insignificant; but is in fact a very valuable tool in teaching your children to preserve wealth.

What does receiving an allowance teach children?

Providing an allowance for children teaches them valuable lessons on learning how to manage and maintain money. In addition, providing your child with an allowance could increase their confidence, help them to appreciate making good financial decisions, and ultimately make them more responsible with their finances. The small decision to provide an allowance to your child (or children) will make an indelible impact on their life's outcome, goals, and financial future.

Although I am a strong proponent for providing your child (or children) with an allowance, I also recognize that there are some parental concerns. One parent asked me, "Doesn't providing an allowance negatively impact a child's development by offering them free money with no expectation of work?" The answer to this question can be summed up by dispelling a common myth: Giving your child an allowance is not about giving your child (or children) handouts or free money with no expectation of work. That's not an allowance. That is called *spoiling your child*. Instead, I believe that when parents provide their children with an allowance, it should be with the expectation that the child is being responsible, doing what they are supposed to do, and being a productive citizen in the home. In other words, no allowance to lazy children!

So, if you provide a child with an allowance, this is not a waste or something that has just negatively impacted the child's development. Instead, you have just made an invaluable investment at an early stage in their growth and development. Moreover, the small decision to give your child (or children) an allowance early on, will greatly impact the decisions that they will make with money and finances early on.

5 Principles in Giving Allowance

1. Give them access to their allowance.

Hands off with your children and their allowance. In other words, don't say "I'm giving you an allowance, but you can't touch it or have access to it until you are 18" because it might be their college fund or a sweet 16 car fund, etc. That is not an allowance. Instead, allow them to have complete access to touch, feel, spend, save, invest, and make errors with money.

Allow them to use the proceeds to set realistic goals and pay off whatever responsibilities they may have and make errors with money early on. This will teach them early on the value of money, the importance of having healthy spending habits, money management skills, how to avoid bad debt by purchasing items that are out of their budget, and allow them to venture out and be productive saving, investing, bill paying, responsible individuals.

Of course, ultimately, the advantage for you and them in doing this is the fact that whatever they do with it, they are still under the guidance and supervision of a parent. This means that if they find themselves having made a bad financial decision, they are likely protected by you and have the ability to seek your guidance and counsel.

2. Let them earn it.

It's healthy to let your children work for an allowance when they become of a certain age. This is healthy because in the real world, there are no handouts. However, be careful because you don't want your child to associate their hard work with only getting paid, but also you want to encourage them to step out and be creative with using their allowance money (e.g., using it to sponsor a game tournament or basketball tournament among friends or local cheerleading competition or open up a lemonade or hotdog stand with their allowance money). These innocent activities will teach them basic lessons about using money to make more money which will indirectly teach them not to strive to just work for someone else, but to create income generating venues for themselves. These types of positive experiences may breed the next generation of entrepreneurs and investors in your children.

In addition, the work that you give your child in exchange for their allowance may be in the form of doing chores around the house like cleaning up, mowing the yard, or washing the dishes. Alternatively, they may be able to earn their allowance by receiving good grades, doing well in school, etc. Therefore, establish positive expectations for your children and allow them to work towards your expectations in exchange for their allowance.

3. Don't give them too much.

Parents please don't make the mistake of giving your children too much. A kid between ages 10-15, should not be receiving an allowance of $50-

$100 despite where you, mom, or dad, or guardian, or grandparent(s) may work. This type of seed is asking for trouble and could cultivate the wrong type of seed in your children and become a problem later down the road. Instead, you want to give your children a modest amount so that they can understand what it means to have to save toward the end goal and then, make tough financial decisions (i.e., whether to spend the $100 allowance they saved for a year on one pair of Nike sneakers and lose it all – or buy $15 sneakers and have money left over for school shopping). If you give them too much, they will never learn these lessons in saving, budgeting, and being disciplined to reach a financial goal. Please, stay away from giving allowances that will make your child overly comfortable.

4. Take advantage of teaching moments.

Children make errors with money and please anticipate them doing so. Please be an open book and talk with them about money and their decisions and the lack of consideration involved. Talk with them about the mistakes they make. It will help them in the long run. Also, encourage them when they do something good with it like paying tithes, giving to charity, and making other healthy spending habits. This positive reinforcement will encourage them to be well rounded and use their resources to benefit others.

5. Encourage them to Tithe.

By making it a requirement that 10% of their allowance automatically goes toward their tithe, you are teaching your child to become a giver. This principle is important because you want your children to grow up knowing that it is important to always first give to God and then to other people in need. This will prevent your child from growing up with an unhealthy and selfish perspective as it relates to money.

How much should I give?

This scale is only meant to guide you in selecting an appropriate amount. Use it as a reference only! Give what you can afford. Please don't go in debt over a child's allowance. All of these amounts are what the child may receive over a two-week period. If you have several children, you may want to down scale these amounts to make it more affordable for you (and may also inadvertently teach your children to use money to work together).

Child's Age	Amount/2 weeks
1	$1
2	$1
3	$1
4	$2.50
5	$2.50
6	$3.00
7	$3.50

8	$4
9	$4.50
10	$5
11	$5.50
12	$6
13	$7
14	$8
15	$10
16	$15
17	$17
18	$20

(Note: This chart should be used as a reference guide only. As a result, if you do not personally believe or think that it is a wise practice to give infants (1-8) money or kids that are able to get jobs (16-18) money, please do not feel obligated by this chart as it is completely up to you.)

5 Suggestions for Parents to Encourage Children To Do When Providing an Allowance:

1. **Encourage** them to pay tithes (10% of their allowance given to their church).
2. **Encourage** them to open up a savings account at a nearby bank.
3. **Encourage** them to open up an online investment account.

4. **Encourage** them to purchase their own snacks for school.
5. **Encourage** them to save towards purchasing clothing, shoes, etc with their allowance money.

8 Things Parents Should <u>NOT</u> Do When Providing an Allowance:

1. **Do not** give them an allowance, but still purchase everything for them.

2. **Do not** give them an allowance, but refuse to let them use it.

3. **Do not** open up a bank account for them.

4. **Do not** open up an online investment account for them.

5. **Do not** force them to do things with their allowance like paying off your bills.

6. **Do not** give them an allowance even though they haven't done any thing to earn it (i.e. household chores, good grades, etc.)

7. **Do not** reward them for poor performance.

8. **Do not** stop giving them an allowance without giving them advanced notice.

Thank you parents, guardians, caretakers, and others for taking out the time to read this chapter on providing an allowance to your children. Giving your children an allowance equips them with a valuable tool that will help open up their eyes to the importance of money management, wealth building, and making smart financial decisions at an early age. It has blessed me to share this information with you. I pray that this insight from me blesses you and your children as well.

A Conversation with the Author:
Receiving an Allowance as a Kid

When I was 7 years old, my mother used to give me $.35 cents every Sunday. The only stipulation was that I put $.10 cents in church and then, could use the rest for myself or buy something from the store. I remember how excited I was at church when the collection plate came around because I had something shinny in my pocket to give. But, what I was most excited about were all of the green one-dollar bills I was able to exchange my shinny pieces of silver for once they had accumulated. The goal of saving $5 became a lesson in saving $10. The goal of saving $10 became a lesson in money management and became $15. The goal of saving $15 became a lesson in making good financial decisions and become $20. And now, I know and help others know the value of money.

FYI: - My mother continued to provide me with an allowance until I got my first job at 16 years old at Winn-Dixie. I remember telling her that I had just got paid at Winn-Dixie and was excited about receiving my allowance. She looked at me and said, "Juan, because you have a job, there's no more allowance for you." And from that day forth, there were no more allowances for me. I pray that this chapter from my life has been able to be a blessing unto you.

Unit Three: X-factors

Chapter XI

X-FACTORS

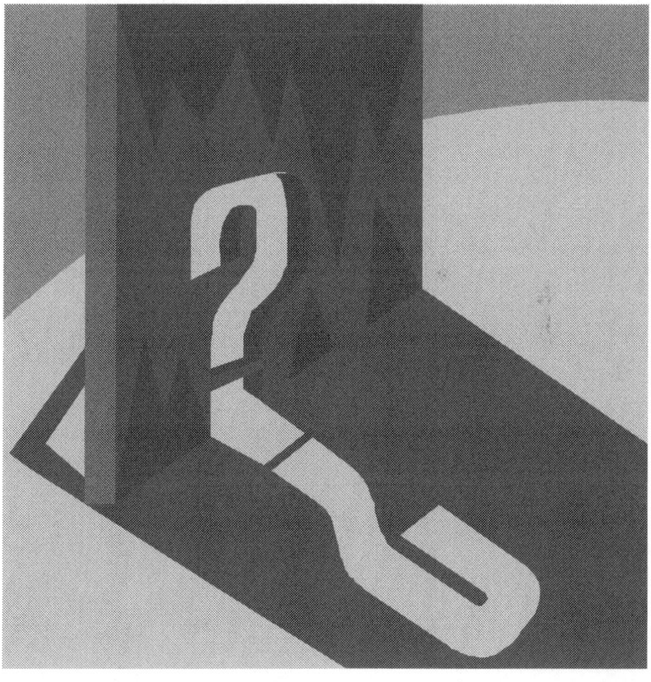

X-FACTORS

"Ideas are funny little things. They don't work unless you do."

Anonymous

"A gift opens the way for the giver and ushers him into the presence of the great."

Proverbs 18:16 (NIV)

When God's purpose (for you), meets His plan (for you). Imagine that your cousin, Crystal, is preparing to give birth to a newborn baby. The entire family is excited about the newborn's arrival, especially your great uncle Teddy that is 97 years old. As the date quickly approaches, your great uncle Teddy suffers a stroke and is now in the hospital in critical condition. Everyone goes to visit uncle Teddy and even in his impaired condition, he is still in good enough spirits to trust God and still be excited about the arrival of that beautiful unborn bundle of joy.

However, realizing that he may not *be around* to see the baby, uncle Teddy promises that he will leave four gifts through his estate to be given to Crystal's baby after he or she is born. These gifts are to serve as an acknowledgement to how much he wanted to be there for the child and also as a final act of appreciation to the person preparing to give birth.

The future gifts are arranged to be given to the baby at his or her *first, ninth, sixteenth, and twenty-third* birthdays.

Sadly, your great uncle Teddy passes away. He leaves in his will directions for his estate to fulfill the promise as he specified by providing four gifts with each of the four selected birthdays of the child. The only disclaimer is that if any gift is not claimed within a year after it is available, it will permanently be forfeited.

Shortly, thereafter a little girl is born, named Gina and through the aid of her parents, she is able to claim gift #1. It is a picture of Uncle Teddy and Crystal with a note that said, "I love you dearly, Teddy." At age nine, she is able to claim gift #2 through her parents. It is a book entitled: *How To Make Your Past, A Blessing To Your Future* and a note from Teddy saying, "This was my favorite book on finance." However, at age sixteen, Gina wants to pick up the gift, but without the aid of her parents, she is unable to claim gift #3 due to juggling a rigorous school schedule and her first job in order to earn enough money towards the purchase of a car. In addition, Gina is involved in a very time consuming relationship with her boyfriend. Consequently, she fails to travel to pick up the gift in a timely fashion. Therefore, her third gift at sixteen was forfeited. Life continues for Gina.

At age twenty-three, Gina is a college graduate and is still busy making her mark on her first full-time job; trying her best to manage bills and expenses; is engaged to be married to her high-school sweetheart, and just doesn't have time to collect her gift from Teddy's estate. Therefore, a second time, she has forfeited her last gift to be received from her late, great uncle Teddy.

Later in life, at age twenty-five, Gina as a young woman, finally gets a break and has sometime to reflect on her life. She decides to journey over to Teddy's estate and retrieve anything from the two late gifts that she never was able to receive through Uncle Teddy. From her efforts, she is able to claim only a final note that was left from Teddy in reference to her third and final gift. The note read:

"Forgive me if I went a little overboard, but I prayed for you before you were born and God reminded me that early on in my late teenage years and early twenties, I struggled to make ends meet. However, after one 'big' break, my life changed with the powerful, life-changing idea that God gave me for my business which ushered open the doors for my life to become much easier. Moreover, for the remainder of my life, I've lived a very comfortable and lavish life. Therefore, I only wanted to make your life a little more convenient for you so you could focus on what was important. I hope you enjoyed seeing the picture of me at age one to always remind you how handsome I was and that family was always a priority. I hope and pray that you actually read the book on finance that you received at age 9 so that you understood that money is great especially when we know what to properly do with it. At age sixteen, I hope that you used the $8,000.00 I left you to purchase the car of your choice so you didn't ever get caught up wasting your time on trying to pay for one of those cars that depreciate by thousands of dollars as soon as you drive it off the lot. Finally, to make sure that you were able to progress debt free, I hope that you enjoyed inheriting my former home in Boston with all my possessions that I left you to inherit. This one gift alone increases your *net worth* so you could do anything you want to do in your life. Loving you from far away, Teddy."

Frozen, Gina dropped the note in awe of just how much she had *let go* by not tapping in to the *gifts* that had been given to her.

Sadly, this is the experience of many people. There are so many people that forfeit their God-given gifts, talents, and abilities by never claiming, and applying them to their life. These gifts were given to them before they were born to make their life much easier. All Gina had to do was make the time to claim her blessings and it would have changed her life tremendously. All you have to do is make the time to pursue the God-given gifts that God gave you before you were born in order to change your life. I like to call these gifts that are sometimes taken for granted, "**X-Factors**." X-Factors are God-given gifts that we can use to earn additional money. 'X' is for the unknown and unlimited potential that we all possess. 'Factors' are elements that contribute to a particular end-goal, result, or outcome.

All people have at least one type of creative gift, talent, ability, and/or X-factor. For some people, they are easy to notice from observing their everyday lives and actions. Thus, if you are the only one that knows how to sing the way you sing that could be one of your X-Factors. Or, maybe anytime you are in a foot race, you always seem to win. This uncanny yet natural speed of yours could be your X-Factor or why don't you consult the bibliography of Olympic superstar and sprinter, Michael Johnson. If this is not your X-Factors, maybe you can sing, write, produce, and orchestrate all genres of music like Kirk Franklin. Or, maybe you are a captivating and encouraging public speaker that makes people want to change their lives for the best like Suzie Orman. Or, maybe you are a genius and can draft blueprints to computer software like Bill Gates. Or, maybe you are witty, encouraging, suggestively creative, and have mastered telling narrative stories about the lives of people through theater, movies, and television like Tyler Perry. Or, maybe you have the gumption to believe that you can transcend people, society norms and customs, and the world we live in to make it a more caring and concerned place by using *hope* like Barack Obama. All of these people have embraced, utilized, and applied their X-Factors through their everyday lives and actions. So, what stops everyone else from reaching his or her X Factors?

5 Walls that Can Stop People From Reaching Their X-Factors & How to Tear the 5 Walls Down

1. The Wall of Being Too Busy!

The Wall of being too busy is when people make the excuse that they do not have enough time due to a variety of reasons. Don't let this stop you! You must be willing to take out some time for yourself. This one small decision could change your life. If this is your wall, you can tear it down by utilizing a day (or time) planner to allocate at least two hours a day for you and/or your X-Factor(s).

2. The Wall of Fear.

The wall of fear is when people allow obstacles that are in or out of their control to become permanent hurdles to stop them from pursuing their goals. This can be a dangerous wall to encounter because fear attempts to permanently keep a person "on the wall" and prevent them from ever pursuing their X-Factor. This wall could appear in many forms (i.e., dealing with criticism, losing friends, finding the money, handling rejection, or dealing with family, etc). The solution to tearing down the wall of fear is having faith that if God gave you the idea, God will see you through. In addition, having the gumption to know that you can step out and overcome this obstacle will cause it to crumble.

Also, anytime you encounter the wall of fear, it confirms that you are closer to your greatness than ever before. As a result, the only reason that this wall has appeared in front of you is because your X-Factor may have the ability to change someone's life (including your own) or do or achieve something that has never been done before. So tear down the wall of fear that is trying to block your life and use its remains to build a highway to reach your goals.

3. The Wall of the Unknown.

The wall of the unknown is apparent when people make the excuse "if I do this, I don't know what's going to happen". Therefore, I 'm not going to do it! The goal of the wall of the unknown is to shut you down by keeping you stagnant and in the same place. But, in order to get around this wall, if you change the semantics in how you view the "unknown," it becomes a source of power and wealth of knowledge that helps you reach your destiny. Moreover, instead of viewing the unknown as being in a dark place that does not have a point of reference to determine success, which inadvertently shuts so many people down; start to view the "unknown" as a learning tool and as a source for personal growth and development. If you can learn to the view this once dark wall in a positive light, anytime you encounter it, the wall of the unknown will offer you a rare opportunity in life to grow. So go past the unknown and expand your horizons by becoming who you were destined to be!

4. The Wall Apathy.

If you have an idea, gift, ability, or solution to a problem, but you don't believe that you should share it because you believe that it's worthless or pointless, you have just encountered the wall of apathy. This wall stops people by making them feel that they shouldn't take action because it's not worth it. This wall also has similar qualities to the wall of fear. However, in order to overcome this wall, it's important to simply step out and try. How do you know that your idea won't be successful unless you give it a shot? Many inventions, business ideas, fashion trends, and books were meaningless until someone introduced them to the world and gave them meaning. Get past this wall and prevent yourself from having life regrets by at least stepping out and giving your dream a try.

5. The Wall of Failure & Frustration

This is when people say, "I tried this before and it didn't work so I'm not trying this again." Just because it didn't work does not mean that its not *destined* to work eventually. In fact, most great leaders and entrepreneurs had to defeat the wall of failure & frustration *many* times. Many successful people were fired from jobs, cut from the team, denied loans, ridiculed by publishers, and rejected in every sense of the word. Yet, they did not lose heart. Instead, they learned from their mistakes, losses, and disappointments; and constantly researched and asked questions to find ways around the obstacles that stood in their way. Don't be frustrated or wallow in failure. Be determined.

So, whatever wall is trying to stop you, tear it down and achieve the greatness of your life! Also, a powerful force that is always able to break down any wall is prayer.

How Can I find my gifts?

If you don't know what your gifts are here are 4 keys to help you to find your X-Factors.

4 Irrefutable Keys to Help You to Find Your X Factors

1. Seek God for His Purpose for Your Life.

This requires you to make the small yet powerful decision to pray and ask God for direction in your life. This is the first option that I pursue whenever I need direction or need to make a decision. Moreover, when it comes to asking God for His guidance in reference to your X-Factor and life, I challenge you to pray as if you were extremely ill or as if someone you knew was on their deathbed. This will require you to humble yourself by getting down on your knees and being completely honest with the Lord about your desire to have Him help you. Prayer can truly open up a person's eyes and give them guidance and direction.

2. Ask Your Momma!

Ask your mother, or father, or someone like your spouse, or grandparents, or friends that know you well. The person that you ask may have some insight about you or your life that you may have never even considered or even thought about as being special. But, that one important thing that this special person decides to reference could in fact be your X-Factor or point you in the direction of it. By asking close family members and/or others what you are good at doing, you may secure valuable information that will lead you to finding your X-Factor.

3. Make Time for Self!

By making time for yourself, you will not only be taking out time to find your X-Factor, but you are exercising a very healthy practice for your life. You can use your newly found time for journaling, reflecting, introspection, relaxing, reading, and being yourself. This time can be especially refreshing if your time is usually preoccupied with life, work, school, family, church, or other time consuming obligations. But how much is enough time? That question depends on you! The point is, take a timeout for you.

4. Dare yourself to Dream.

Focus on who you are and what you are capable of achieving! Take yourself back to that place in your subconscious where you can vividly remember what you truly wanted from life. Or, alternatively that one dream you wanted to accomplish that you always knew you were capable of doing, but never accomplished. Without allowing yourself to feel any frustration from those past dreams that you did not achieve, write those things down because these acknowledgements could in fact be your X-Factors.

Now, determine which dreams still seem relevant to your current goals and write out a plan to accomplish them. Remember, there's no harm in looking back, especially if you can use your past experiences to move forward in life.

So, stop burying yourself underneath your busy schedule! Try implementing these keys in your everyday life. They will help you to better understand *who you are* in lieu of how God made you. They will also help you to unlock and wield the powerful gifts that you were born *ready to handle*. I pray that this insight from my life has been able to be a blessing unto you.

<u>A Conversation with the Author:</u>
When a person allows their gifts to shine, phenomenal things happen.

When a person allows their gifts to shine, phenomenal things happen. Will a person's gifts, talents, abilities, and ideas really make room for them? The answer to this question can be seen through the unique lives and testimonies of *once everyday people* like Tyler Perry, Oprah Winfrey, Michael Jordan, Tiger Woods, Bill Gates, Donald Trump, and Barack Obama. Maybe, one day we may all strive to be as big as these successful individuals. But, I am almost certain that many of them may have encountered some of the same uncertainty that many of us face today in our everyday lives. But then, something may have happened that remarkably changed their life—maybe it was through the course of putting together a play that no one showed up for; or talking through a microphone without any listeners; or being cut from a basketball team; or not being able to connect the swing with the golf ball; or looking at the computer and not understanding the code; or dreaming of owning a high-rise building without the money to purchase it; or having hope for the country and being the only one. Maybe, these great modern day heroes had to first lose, live in obscurity and negative situations, be consumed by dark defeating clouds, and deal with depressing circumstances in order to get to the point that they refused to allow their position to stop them. So they took action by stepping out (or be pushed out) in spite of what it looked like. They kept at it again and again and it changed their life forever. Sometimes, the best and only way to have one's X-Factors to come out is by being willing to step out and not look back in spite of how negative or dark things may appear. But step out and shine and watch your gift phenomenally make room for you. I pray that this insight from me has been able to be a blessing unto you.

Chapter XII

Cultivating Your X-Factor

Cultivating Your X-Factor

"God gives us dreams a size too big so that we can grow in them."

Anonymous

Observation: Although David had three stones, it took only one to slay Goliath.

Cultivating your X-Factors starts with believing in you and being willing to step out. In the Biblical story of Samuel found in the Old Testament of the Bible, we learn that before David was known as the great King David and "a man after God's own heart," he was only little David, Joseph's youngest son that no one expected much if anything from him outside of being a shepherd. But David was willing to put it all on the line and step out when the time came. When Goliath, a nine feet tall giant, showed up and threatened David's people, the Israelites, he decided to take action. Could you imagine seeing and hearing this young, skinny boy step up to this nine-feet tall man and challenge him with only a sling shot in hand? I'm sure if our current world of fantasy football could make a prediction on who would win between the Little Shepard and the Giant, all bets would have went on the giant. David could have ran, turned away, or even changed his mind, but he did not. After seeking God, he made the goal of defeating Goliath his top priority and in spite of ridicule from his family, friends, and people, he stood his ground. The Bible tells us that David pulled one of three stones from his pocket and placed it inside of his slingshot. Once it was inside, he wielded it around and around, and around and released it. He realized that he had done more than just release a small angular shaped rock from a slingshot, but he was metaphorically releasing himself to God to shape his life and future. The rock would hit Goliath and knock him out cold. David then advanced to complete the task at hand. After slaying this Giant, this small skinny, boy had propelled himself into God's destiny for his life. And the great news is that you can do the same!

3 Powerful Beliefs that Helped to Cultivate David's X-Factor

1. **He had the faith to believe and the boldness to step out.**

David possessed a powerful combination of X-Factors that we all possess, but often don't apply to our lives. David had so much faith until his X-Factor may have been the fact that he trusted that God would work things out. Alternatively, his X-Factor could have been that David was very bold about pursing what he believed he should be doing. This powerful combination enabled David to defeat the giant *problems, conflicts, obstacles, and hurdles* that attempted to prevent him from reaching his destiny. Next time a giant shows up in your life in utilizing your X-Factor, think of David and how his faith and boldness changed his life.

2. He didn't allow what he looked like to stop him!

It's sad to believe that what stops some people from achieving their goal is in what they look like or where they come from (i.e., their race, clothes, car, neighborhood, or parents). They believe the stereotypes displayed on television that limit them based on their profile and those things become a self-fulfilling prophecy. The reality is that none of these things have anything to do with your purpose and/or your X-Factor. Thus, don't let image stop you! David was successful because he knew he was blessed, he believed in himself, and saw himself as the person he was destined to become—a King. So be confident in your present circumstances and instead of looking in the mirror, look deeper in your heart and start seeing yourself as the person you are destined to become.

3. **He didn't let family or friends stop him**

Sometimes, it easy to give up when family and/or friends are not on your side. There were times in David's life where he also did not have his family or friends on his side. But he did not allow this to stop him. What distinguished David is the fact that despite who was or was not supporting him, he continued to affirm himself as being born a winner, successful, and victorious and pushed toward his goal—defeating Goliath. If family members, friends, and/or others that you really admire are not on your side, this is not the end of the world. Simply, start reaffirming yourself as being born a winner, successful, and victorious and push towards achieving your goals.

Moreover, these three powerful beliefs helped David to cultivate his X-Factor and pursue his goals. Use them to be empowered to achieve your goals.

But I'm not David, he had a Weapon! What do I have?

Weapon? David's weapon was only a *sling shot*! He had neither a gun, nor a bazooka, nor a tank to win against the giants in his life. But all he had was a slingshot with 3 small stones in his pocket; and all it took was just one of those stones to win, which changed his life. But you have something much bigger than David's sling shot—you have an idea. And how many ideas does it take to change a person's life? Just **one**. Everyone has something that they can do to win and change the direction of their life. I pray that this chapter from me has been able to be a blessing unto you.

A Conversation with the Author:

Salvaging Your Dream

Maybe you used to imagine seeing yourself on television; or singing alongside superstars; or designing the latest trends; or walking confidently alongside presidential dignitaries and world-leaders; or curing that disease; helping out that person in the courtroom; or designing a place as beautiful as Michelangelo's Sistine Chapel; or bringing a riveting message before that congregation. Despite where life has taken you, try to find ways that you can salvage your dreams and X-factors and make them apart of your present.

X-Factor Illustrations

Here are some illustrations to help you salvage your dream and/or X-Factor:

1. Athletics. If basketball, football, baseball, tennis, golf, cheerleading, or some other sporting venue was your top priority and if you are past the point of playing, maybe you can consider coaching, becoming a sportscaster, referee, or becoming a sports agent. You could even use another creative X-Factor to design special gear, technology or better equipment to solve a problem that currently exists for athletes in your field of interest.

2. Musician or Singer. Write and record your own music. Hire a lawyer to copyright it. Then, hire someone to build a website and/or broadcast your work on YouTube.com. Also, contact local restaurants and offer to play during the weekends for exposure. Advertise and play at weddings, parties, and events. Record a CD and sell it through your website and to others.

3. Writer. Consider starting a writer's website to post samples of your work and promote yourself. Buy your own domain name (e.g., www.JuanChisholm.com) and promote the site among your friends and family as a way of getting exposure for your work.

4. Dancer. Offer dance lessons out of your home or rent a dance studio to teach lessons. Make your own dance video or website for enthusiasts. Invent a product line to offer to other dancers or become an expert and speak at various dance conferences, schools, and functions about your particular area of expertise.

5. Orator. Volunteer at schools and with community groups as a motivational speaker. Share your knowledge and expertise to benefit others during your spare time. Consider making a DVD and CDs that you can promote and sell at your events for extra income.

6. Photographer, Web Designer, Videographer. Post ads on www.Craigslist.org and in local bulletins and papers advertising your availability to do freelance work on the side. Find books in the library to assist you in setting up your hourly fees and doing business as an independent contractor.

7. Gamer. Consider looking up a graphic design program at a local community college or university and take classes in design to create your own games. You could also compete in tournaments or host your own for extra income.

8. Consultant. If you have specialized knowledge or experience in a certain field, start a business and solicit businesses in lieu of your specialized knowledge as a consultant that can help their business. Also, research independent contractor agreements to help your business to establish itself apart from the companies that it represents.

9. Other interests. Enroll in a community college or part time graduate program to learn more about your interest. Contact local libraries for listings of the free classes they offer. Consider hiring a professional in the industry to give you private lessons at an hourly rate if you cannot commit to a full-time program. Research books on your topic of interest in the library and find other people through trade associations and interest groups that are doing what you desire to do.

Remember, in all of these endeavors, to protect yourself. Consult with a lawyer to make sure that you are operating legally and to protect your ideas so that someone else does not misappropriate them (e.g., copyrights, trademarks, and patents for your original works). I pray that this chapter from me has been able to be a blessing unto you.

Chapter XIII

The Power of Teamwork: Combining X-Factors with *Synergy*

The Power of Teamwork: Combining X-Factors with Synergy

"If you are afraid of your ideas, you are afraid of yourself!"

Juan Phillip Chisholm

Every single instrument has its own unique sound. When you hear the melodic sound of the piano, it sounds like a piano. When you hear the harmonious sound of a clarinet, it sounds like a clarinet. When you hear the classical sound of the violin, it sounds like a violin. When you hear the bright sound of a trumpet, it sounds like a trumpet. When you hear the rhythmic sound of timpani, it sounds like a timpani. Individually played, these instruments have their own unique sound. But it's when you combine the sounds of the instruments that you have the potential to create a band, or a symphony, or an orchestra. This display of synergy is also what inspired the lives of some of the greatest musical geniuses like: Ludwig van Beethoven, Wolfgang Mozart, Duke Ellington, Nadia Boulanger and others.

But imagine, what could happen if you were to combine **your** X-Factors with the right group of people? What would you all be able to create? What would you all be able to do? What could stop you from discovering the cure for cancer; inventing a new, affordable fuel; forming an NBA Championship Team; building or buying a successful business, transforming a high-crime community into a much safer one, and more! There are infinite treasures to be found awaiting the right combination of X-Factors and synergy to chisel them into existence.

However, if these musical sounds (X-Factors) would have never been combined with the synergy from the right people, then these great composers along with their great works of art may have never been born or left their mark on society. When you combine the gifts of others, you are igniting the fires of greatness inside of you and the team that you are collaborating with. The synergy that is formed can be described as life changing and powerful. So, what are you waiting for?

How can I link with the right people in order to find the right synergy?

Here's a twofold process to link you with the right people to find the right synergy.

1. Know what you are looking for.

In order to link with the right people, you must first know what you are looking for. If I am a motivational speaker, I am **not** looking for someone that can teach me how to speak, but I may be looking for a web-designer that will help me to reach new audiences. Alternatively, if I am a singer, I am likely looking for someone that can help me to record at a music studio. The point is, by knowing what you are looking for, it will help to save you time and connect you to the right people.

How do you know what you need? By thinking of the elements that are missing to achieve your goal. Most enterprises require a **tangible** or **intangible** good or service that will be offered to the public and then, individuals that function around it. Tangible goods or services come in the form of goods or services that react to your basic senses (i.e., seeing, hearing, touching, tasting, and smelling). An example would be selling lemonade as a product and washing cars as a service. These are tangible goods and services. Intangible goods and services come in the form of selling a concept, or an idea, or providing some form of mental assurance like "comfort," or "safety."

In bridging it all together, your X-factor might lead you to start a benevolent program in the neighborhood that will decrease crime in the community. Decreasing crime is an intangible service. In order to achieve this goal, you will likely need to link up with: (1) the local police department to find out about available programs, policies, procedures, and services in your area that may affect your group in achieving its goal. (2) You may also want to get other neighbors involved, which will create a sense of unity and community accountability.

(3) You will need to have a reliable secretary or someone that possesses clerical skills that can record the minutes from each meeting and distribute them likely in the form of email and mail to members and non-members living in the community, local police department contact, and all other parties involved. (4) If there is any money involved (dues collected, receipts distributed, revenue received, expenditures purchased), you will need to link with a trustworthy and reliable person that possess accounting skills and have them to operate as a Treasurer for the organization. (5) Lastly, to expand the scope of your organization, you may want to have a liaison established with the city leaders of that particular district, local churches and community leaders, and school leaders in that area so that you can all work in unison to achieve the goal of decreasing crime and promoting a safer community. By connecting with the right people, the display of synergy created will help you to achieve your goal.

2. Go to right places!

If you want to find the people with the right synergy to help you, go to the places where powerful minds congregate. Go to reputable places like the libraries, churches, chambers of commerce, local trade organizations, college campuses, and others places where people are doing what you want to do. Interestingly, business owners are usually members of the chamber of commerce and attend trade shows and exhibitions; musicians can be found at music stores and concerts; community leaders may be found at city hall meetings and other political events; attorneys are found at court houses, law libraries, and bar association meetings; resources and information may be found at the library or your local college or university. Going to these places, may help you to find someone to align yourself with to achieve your goals.

Also, please visit the following amazing websites that may help you to link with the right people in order to find the right synergy.

- www.score.org
- www.craigslist.com

Once you have linked with the right people, here are *10 Easy Ways* that you can benefit from by combining your X-Factors with the right synergy.

10 Easy Ways that You Can Benefit by Combining Your X-Factors with the Right Synergy

1. Surround yourself with positive people that believe in you.

Having positive people around you that believe in you is very important when it comes to doing anything. There are numerous advantages in having this important group of people around you. Some of them will help to keep you positive and confident in spite of what you may encounter. In addition, positive people have a way of birthing even bigger ideas in you beyond what you may have ever thought of or ever considered. By surrounding yourself with positive people, you are on your way to finding the right synergy!

2. Ask for feedback on your idea from one or two trusted people.

In Mathew 7:6 (NIV), the Bible has a story that reminds people not to throw their pearls away to pigs. What this means is that if you don't trust the person, don't share your idea with them. If you do this, you are throwing your pearls (valuable ideas) to someone that may actually be a pig (someone that will either steal your idea or try to discourage you from pursuing it). The purpose of asking for feedback or constructive criticism is to help fine-tune an already good idea. Also only share your idea with trusted people like a mentor and/or someone that is actually able to understand what you are proposing. Their constructive criticism could be the X-Factor you need along with their feedback as the necessary synergy to take your idea to new heights.

3. Surround yourself with people that are smarter than you.

This group of people is not the people that you have to share your ideas with in-depth, but this group serves an important purpose in helping to expand your idea. A fish can only grow as big as the size of its bowl. Therefore, if you are the smartest person in your group, then you can't grow anymore. Expand your network and surround yourself with people that are smarter than you. This will keep your ideas fresh and you constantly expanding.

4. Find people that may have some experience in doing what you are doing.

By finding people that have some experience in what you are doing, you can ask them to be your advisor or mentor. This small simple decision could in fact change the way you view your X-Factor and ultimately, change your life.

5. Create a list of people that can benefit from what you are doing.

Create a list of people that can benefit from what you are doing. This list could become a goldmine for business prospects or clients to solicit your goods or services. However, before *digging for gold* through your list of people, please be sure to have a plan in action.

6. Start off small (only handle about one or two people at a time).

By starting off small, this will allow you to perfect your system and benefit from learning from your early mistakes before having the pressure of an influx of clients.

7. Read magazines and information on your X-Factor, trade, or related ideas.

Reading magazine and other information on your X-Factors, trades, or similar ideas will keep you current. For example, if your interest is in boxing, you should be current on the latest material relevant to that industry. You should be a member of the noted boxing societies, subscribe to any boxing magazines or journals (or read them for free at a local library if you cannot afford them), remain current with websites featuring boxing news, and read books informing you of the latest information on past and present boxers. If your X-factor involves technology, subscribe to technological publications, research the industry, and pursue degrees and educational venues related to your interests (computers, internet, new technological gadgets, etc.). Keep current with the information!

8. Utilize your public library system.

This is a place that will help you build off of your synergy because the library is one of the few places where you can consistently get training (outside of school or college) usually free of charge. By taking these classes and other local classes in your area, you may be able to meet someone (network) that will help you to achieve your goal. Most modern libraries offer free classes, books on your X-Factor, trade associations, magazines related to your X-factor, as well as DVDs and video collections. Take advantage of using your public library system!

9. Pray and ask God for Direction.

This is an important step that people often allow to slip through the cracks. Always be willing to seek God for direction in prayer. God may lead you to try a non-conventional means of achieving your goal that may be the key to the success that you are looking for. But, after God gives it to you, it's up to you to trust Him and try it. Seek God in prayer for direction!

10. Be willing to let people go that are <u>dead weight</u>.

If you have people around you that are putting you or your ideas down, discouraging you from your dreams, or constantly reminding you of your past mistakes, these people are **all dead weight**. Let them go now! Don't ever be afraid to let people go in your life that are trying to pull you down! Cut them from your life and trust that God will give you new friends that will inspire and push you into your destiny. Remember, in order to soar with eagles, you cannot hang out with buzzards. Let dead weight go and you will be amazed at how high you can fly!

I pray that this chapter from me has been able to be a blessing unto you.

A Conversation with the Author:
Let Dead Weight Go and You Will Be Amazed at How High You Can Fly

In business and in my personal life, I've learned that if there is anything that will take you down quickly, it's holding on to dead weight. When I first tried to write my first book, I was connected with what I believed to be an exciting group of acquaintances. They were good people, but only relished in the thought of writing books, instead of the work that goes into actually writing a book. After some time had passed, and my goal had not been met, I was led to part ways with this group. Once, I changed circles and linked with a much more positive and happy group, in less than six months, through God's blessing, I had crafted my first manuscript. And within another six months, my first book: How To Make Your Past, A Blessing To Your Future had been published.

If the people around you are not trying to push you onward and upward towards your goal, you have to be willing to let them go. You can lose it all for the sake of dead weight that is not even benefiting you. We hold onto them because we feel like we have invested so much into those relationships and we fear what our life will be like without them. However, I challenge you to make the right decision and let go of dead weight. Then, surround yourself with the right combination of people with the right synergy that will help you to achieve your goal. I pray that this insight from me has been able to be a blessing unto you.

Chapter XIV

Bartering X-Factors For Services

Bartering X-Factors for Services

"If you aim at nothing, you'll hit it every time."
Anonymous

If all you had was a red, small paper clip to barter, what do you believe you could and/or would receive from exchanging it? What known and unknown treasures could be unlocked with every exchange? Well, Kyle MacDonald answered that question with an amazing real life story that details his journey of exchanging a small, red paper clip and what he received in return. Ultimately, he bartered that red paperclip over the course of 14 trades into a small *key*. This key was for the door of a home he had bartered for in Canada. Wow! For more about Kyle, please visit his website: http://oneredpaperclip.blogspot.com/ to learn more about his amazing story. If Kyle MacDonald's red, small paperclip could earn him the key to his own home in Canada, just image what bartering your X-Factors will do for you?

What Does It Mean to Barter?

When you barter, you are negotiating the exchange of goods or services for other goods or services.

How Does Bartering Contribute to Your X-Factors?

Bartering can definitely contribute to your X-Factor goals because it can save you money by giving you the benefit of someone's gift or other special item without using your money. In addition, you can use your X-Factor as a means of exchanging services for cash or as a means of exchanging it for other services (e.g., baking a sweet potato pie in exchange for a relative babysitting your children or you driving your car in exchange for a friend cooking dinner).

10 Tips that will Help You to Barter Your Services or Goods

1. Make your safety your first concern!

Anytime you barter, always make sure that your safety is your first priority by always bartering from a safe distance. This could be achieved by following these safety precautions:

- #1: Try using the mail whenever you can to complete your bartering transactions.

- #2: Never give out your personal home address. Instead, use a P.O. Box address.

- #3: Never allow or agree to meet a complete stranger at your home or meet them at their home. Instead, always meet at a central location that is highly populated (e.g., shopping mall, inside a gym, at a school, inside your church, or at a local restaurant or café' that you are familiar with).

- #4: And if you do meet at one of the aforementioned places mentioned in #3, always take a buddy along with you to further ensure your safety instead of going alone.

- #5: In addition, have mobile accountability partners (like a spouse, parent, grandparent, best friend, etc.) that know you very well and will call you at a specified time to confirm that you are safe. The mobile accountability person (unlike the buddy) is not physically with you and as a result should know the specifics of who/what/when/where/ and why you are meeting with the person you plan to barter with. For example, my wife is often my accountability partner and as such, she would know that I am meeting, "Mr. John Doe to complete a barter for the exchange of my Seminole Cap for an SAT Book on December 4 at 12:06 pm in Starbucks located off Tennessee Street. The meeting should last no more than 10 minutes so she can call me @ 12:16pm." This type of accountability further ensures your safety.

- ❑ #6: Never barter personal services such as babysitting, dog sitting, private massages, washing, cleaning, lessons, or anything similar that requires you to go into the home of a complete stranger. Instead, have them meet you in a central location as mentioned in #3. Also, be sure to have a buddy along with you and your accountability partner on stand by.

Furthermore, by making safety, your first concern, you are free to barter!

2. Have Tenacity.

By having tenacity, always barter for the unexpected. Even if you do not think that it is obtainable, try to barter for it anyway. You never know what might be the outcome. Who would have known that a small, red paperclip would have been upgraded to a home in Canada?

3. Set a Bartering End Goal.

By setting a bartering end goal, you are determining, what it is that you ultimately want to receive from your bartering (e.g., roller blades, Iron Fist comic book #14, a Macintosh computer, a Chrysler Sebring convertible, etc). By setting a bartering end goal, it transforms bartering from being an endless pursuit into a dynamic contest towards a specific accomplishment.

4. Be willing to travel.

By being willing to travel, you are expanding the area that can be used to achieve your bartering goals. The larger the area, the more likely you will find someone that is willing to trade with you. Be sure to rely on the Internet, email, and mail as a tool to make your bartering dreams into a reality.

5. Never mention money but give a receipt.

When you barter, you are exchanging a something for a something. As a result, bartering does not require you to give the person you are bartering with money, but merely the "something" that you are trying to exchange. However, in order to protect your exchange and make sure that it is a permanent one, give the person a receipt that records the transaction. For example, a receipt may record the following transaction as "Mr. John Doe exchanged a Sony VHS Recorder with serial number: 12345 for a six-string bass guitar from Ms. Jane Doe." This bill of sale in the absence of money may protect your exchange later down the road.

6. Be Upfront and Honest with People.

Be upfront and honest with people about what you are bartering! Give honest and accurate descriptions of your goods or services and their value. It is also okay to add creativity in your descriptions along with your honesty. For example, "This is an old Winnie the Pooh teddy bear that I have had since 1981. Although it has no magical powers, it did guard me from the Boogieman when I was a child. It's worth something that will make me laugh so hard that I cry."

7. Keep a Record.

Keep an updated record or list of all of your X-Factors and/or items that you have and what they were exchanged for. This could become very useful as you can later use it to determine minimum limitations and maximum expectations for the goods and/or services that you barter. For example, if you design a website for a business lawyer, he/she may exchange you up to 10 hours of legal advice on your web design company. This insight may become helpful in setting a minimum expectation next time you meet with a similar client to bargain with.

8. Barter Legally.

Make sure that whatever you barter, you are doing it in a legal capacity. If you have questions on the legality of your bartering arrangement(s), please consult an attorney that practices in your state regarding your specific dealings before continuing with your bartering activities.

9. <u>Stay Away</u> from Unethical or Illegal Exchanges.

During the course of your bartering, if anyone ever asks you to do anything that is either illegal or inappropriate (e.g., prostitution, violent acts, drug and/or alcohol related activities) please **stay away from this person**! This type of conduct is improper and should be reported to the police **immediately**!

10. Try to always do a good job!

When you barter, try to do a good job. Your reputation still counts! Always give, act and operate in a way that is professional, ethical, and legal.

What are some Creative Things that People Commonly Barter?

Here are some creative things that have been bartered:

- Speaking at a college conference for free in order to meet others that would pay you to speak and receive an ongoing contract to sell your items in the college bookstore.

- Babysitting a younger brother or sister in order to have access to the car on the weekend.

- A restaurant donating food to a charitable organization's conference in exchange for being able to distribute pamphlets regarding the restaurant's catering services to the conference attendees.

- A retail store donating apparel to an entrepreneur hosting a fashion show in exchange for an advertisement promoting the store in the program booklet.

- Speaking at a conference and have them make a donation to your favorite charity.

- Playing the piano for a friend's wedding reception for free in exchange for giving them a wedding gift.

3 Partnerships Established Through Bartering

1. Ask the person to give you customer referrals from their business.

2. Ask the person for a free sample in exchange for you patronizing their business. For example, having a restaurant agree to sponsor a free dinner for your group in exchange for you hosting a rehearsal dinner or other event at their restaurant.

3. Ask the person for free hotel rooms at their hotel or conference facility in exchange for you

agreeing to do all of your events at their location.

Always look for creative ways that you can enhance your bartering. If a small, red paperclip could earn Mr. Kyle MacDonald the keys to a home, imagine what doors your creativity can open for you. I pray that this insight from me has been able to be a blessing unto you.

A Conversation with the Author:

Bartering for College Students

In college, learn to barter everything! It can be a very effective means of delivering in college. Usually, in college towns (or smaller communities of people), there is an abundance of intelligent and talented people that will eagerly barter with you in exchange for something that they may want from you. It was in such an environment that I bartered to have one of my first business websites created. In exchange, I agreed to refer clients to the web designer's new business and compensate him with a one time nominal fee of $100.00. After our bartering, we both walked away feeling like winners. I am very thankful to God for having this experience. I pray that this chapter of my life is able to add a blessing unto yours.

Chapter XIII

Scholarships

Scholarships

"Winning is not just about taking chances. It's about having a good attitude despite the outcome."
Juan Phillip Chisholm

Having time on your side is a valuable X-Factor when it comes to pursuing scholarships. This is one common X-Factor that full-time students on all levels possess. In this chapter, you will learn how to use that time effectively to earn money from scholarships and other opportunities.

What about having good grades?

Having good grades is an awesome accomplishment and very commendable! It proves that you went to school, worked hard, and did the things in school that you were supposed to do. Usually, state specific merit scholarships honor students that earn good grades. Congratulations, if you were or will be one of them because these students are often times awarded state scholarships!

Fortunately, scholarships are not just available for students with stellar grades. There are a plethora of scholarships available for all types of students and for a bevy of different reasons. The focus of this chapter will help all students to earn scholarships regardless of the grades you made in school. The only perquisite that is needed to establish your eligibility in searching for the scholarships in this chapter is 1) having the time and 2) being diligent in your pursuit of them. So if you don't have the grades, then that's not a problem. Just be diligent and use your time wisely to pursue the insight from this chapter and I am sure that your pursuit will lead you to free money.

How can I use Time as an X-Factor to earn scholarship money?

1. Organize your scholarship pursuit.

In order to organize your scholarship pursuit, you must at least be cognizant of the following 3 types of scholarship categories:

- **National**
- **State**
- **Local**

National Scholarships are usually found via online scholarships and databases. They are usually open to anyone living in the country that they are offered.

State Scholarships are usually circulated in the form of *State Specific Scholarships* that are often awarded to the top 10% (or top 20%) of students based upon

Grade Point Average (GPA). Many colleges also award state specific scholarships.

Local Scholarships are scholarships available in your immediate area. These scholarships are the ones offered specifically for people living in your city or local community.

2. Know which one you should pursue first.

After asking yourself which scholarship category to pursue first, the answer is likely the category that will be easiest for you to acquire.

State Scholarships:

If you are among the top 10% (or 20%) of your class, you should first start off by finding out if you qualify for state scholarship programs. Visiting your high school's guidance counselors, or college's financial aid officers, and/or contacting your state's department of education can easily achieve this. If you qualify, be sure to complete any necessary forms and/or other prerequisites and you are on your way to having all or at least some of your college education funded. Please consult with one of the aforementioned school officers and visit the following websites as a reference:

- http://www.financialaidfinder.com

- http://www.financialaidfinder.com/financial-aid/financial-aid-programs/state-sponsored-programs/

Local & National Scholarships

If you do not meet the criteria for state scholarships, by default, try to find money for National and Local Scholarships.

Which One Should I Apply for First between National Scholarships and Local Scholarships?

When left with the choice of applying for national or local scholarships, start applying for the local scholarships. Here are 6 tips to help you to find local scholarships and earn money from them.

5 Powerful Tips to Help You to Find Local Scholarships & Earn Money From Them.

1. It's in your ASSOC.

Start your scholarship search for local scholarships by visiting the *"ASSOC."* section in your local phone book. This section will feature various *Associations* in your area that may offer scholarships.

Contact these groups and ask them if they have a scholarship. If so, ask them if they will mail/email/or allow you to pick-up an application. Be as polite as possible; first impressions count. The person that may have answered the phone may in fact be on the scholarship committee and as a result may have a vote in determining the scholarship recipient. Therefore, show as much respect, professionalism, and deference to this person as this decision may translate to possible feedback on your behalf and you reaping the scholarship award.

In addition, even if you do not receive the scholarship packet or they have already given out the award, be sure to mail them a thank you card so that they can remember you next time. Please visit the following other areas of the phonebook and adhere to the same procedure as mentioned above: "CLUBS," "ORGANIZATIONS," "TRADES," and other similar sections.

2. Apply for the ones that are closer to your home first.

Apply for scholarships closer to your home (or area that you live in) first and work your way out. Local scholarships in your community may give scholarship priority to local students that live and go to school in the area. Apply for the scholarships in your community first and then get your application to other areas. Also, if you have friends, family members, or members of your church that are good standing members of the organization, it never hurts to mention to them that you are applying for their organization's scholarship and ask if they have any advice for you. However, do not ask them for any unethical favors such as selecting you for the award simply because you know them.

3. Visit your local school and look for student organization or other groups that award scholarships funds.

Find out the criteria to apply for the award. Let the club sponsor know that you are interested in the award. Apply for it! You never know, these organizations may open up the doors to your scholarship blessing.

4. Try to find out about local scholarships for volunteers in your area.

Look for voluntary scholarship awards. You may be able to find out about these from your local school counselor or other community groups that are involved with your school. Alternatively, you may be able to find out about these scholarships through local community service organizations or service groups in your area or at your local college or university.

5. Go and Apply for Scholarships at Conferences

Find out about conferences and other similar activities in your area and if they have a local scholarship. Find out how to apply for their scholarship and apply for it. You will be amazed that several students don't apply for these types of scholarships. This may work in your favor.

After you complete these tasks, move to National Scholarships.

How do I find National Scholarships and when should I apply for them?

In order to find national scholarships, please visit the following websites:

- http://www.fastweb.com
- http://www.scholarshipexperts.com/
- http://www.brokescholar.com/

Apply for them before they reach their scholarship deadline. All of these websites should be free to sign up for. Use them to apply for all the scholarships that you have time to apply for. Also, be sure to especially make time for the scholarships that require essays since few students apply for them.

Is there anyway to ensure that I will receive a scholarship?

No, there is not a way to ensure that you will receive a scholarship. However, there are several things that you can do in order to increase your chances of receiving one. Here are 3 ways to increase your chances of receiving a scholarship.

3 Ways of Increasing Your Chances of Receiving a Scholarship

1. Always Include A Resume

With every scholarship application, always include a resume with a cover letter that is tailored to the specific scholarship award. Don't be bashful. Be sure to tell them about everything that you have done. For example, be sure to include things like: subjects that you tutor, languages that you can speak, computer skills, foreign countries that you have traveled, summer jobs or internships, volunteer hours, and leadership positions held in school, church, and other involvements.

2. Add at least three additional letters of recommendation.

Add at least three additional letters of recommendation over what the scholarship requires. For example, if the scholarship does not ask for letters of recommendation, as a default, include three. However, if the scholarship does ask for at least 2 letters of recommendation, include 5. The exception is if the application explicitly requests that you do not include additional papers.

3. **Make sure that your application is neat and well organized.**

Make sure that your application is neat and well organized. It is a joy for a person reviewing a scholarship application to look over a neat application. However, when your application is neither neat nor well organized, your accomplishments can easily be overlooked and/or your application not be taken seriously. For example, make sure that you print your resume on *resume paper* (32lb premium weight linen paper with 100% cotton or similar paper sold at office supply stores); make sure that you type or print out your application instead of handwriting it; that the paper you use is not crinkled, nasty-smelling, or has spills, or other unnecessary markings; that there were no streaks in the printing due to your ink cartridge needing to be refilled or replaced. By making sure that these elements are addressed, your application will look very neat and well organized.

Ways to Save on Postage

Mail your scholarship materials using the *Forever Stamp* from the U.S. Post Office. It is called the Forever Stamp because you can buy it at today's price and use it in the future without paying extra even when the price of the same stamp has gone up. Contact your local post office for more information. I pray that this insight from me has been a blessing unto you.

A Conversation with the Author:

No School Loans. No School Debts.

My wife and I have never received any loans for school. In high school, she used the extra time that she had during the course of her senior year to apply for 20 college scholarships (local, state, and national). She received several of the scholarships that she had applied for from churches, community groups, civic organizations, and from Florida State University. She used her scholarship money to pay for college and continued to apply for new scholarships as a student. Then, as a college student, she received a foreign language scholarship, which allowed her to study abroad for free in Spain and Italy for a summer. She also received room and board from a scholarship that gave her free housing and meals for the remainder of college. She worked on campus and used her X-Factor as a musician to earn addition income to pay for school. As a result, she graduated from college debt free.

In law school, she became an entrepreneur when she stepped out using one of her X-factors to start a college apparel retail store (www.famutshirts.com). She also bought a house that she used as a rental property, and still used her additional time and status as a student to earn academic scholarships to graduate debt free (without credit cards, student loans, etc).

My story is the same. In high school, I applied for several local and national scholarships and received a number of them. I also received several leadership and community service awards. In addition, I worked at my college dorm as a Resident Assistant in exchange for free housing and meals. At the same time, I also worked for a research center and budgeted the money that I earned to pay for school. Although it took some sacrifice and smart financial planning, I graduated debt free.

After graduating from college, I wanted to continue my education debt free. I decided to use my X-Factor by using the book sales of the second edition of "How To Make Your Past A Blessing To Your Future" to pay for a program in Strategic Finance that I completed at the Harvard Business School in Boston.

With the favor of God, and implementing the financial strategies included within Investitude, my wife and I both graduated debt free and you can do the same. I pray that this chapter of my life is able to be a blessing unto yours.

Unit Four: Entrepreneurship

Chapter XVI

Entrepreneurship

Entrepreneurship

"Never be afraid to do something new. Remember, amateurs built the ark; professionals built the titanic."

Anonymous

The first time I stepped out to pursue a business idea as an entrepreneur, I failed. This failure served as a bittersweet moment in my life because on the one hand, I wanted to keep the business going. I believed we had a great idea, I enjoyed the freedom of business ownership, and the things that I learned as an entrepreneur excited me. But on the other hand, I had to respect the fact that our business funds were almost completely depleted, I had loaned my own personal resources to the business and had lost them, my support team had dwindled, and our purpose for going into business had become skewed. Although I was an entrepreneur with a great idea, I had to let the business go. However, in the process, I learned some valuable lessons about entrepreneurship. I learned that anyone could be an entrepreneur if you have an idea, time, and financial resources. But, I also learned that in order to become an effective entrepreneur, it takes becoming a mountain climber.

What does it take to be an Effective Entrepreneur?

To become an effective entrepreneur, it requires you to become a mountain climber. Mountain climbers are revered for their diligence in pursuing their goal of reaching the top of the mountain despite the numerous obstacles that they face along the climb. During their climb, they often encounter the cold realities of falling rocks (or ice), snow, bad weather, and altitude. All of these obstacles have the potential to knock the mountain climber down. Yet, the mountain climber holds firm to his/her goal. Their drive pushes them forward and up the mountain of opportunity until they reach its peak.

Effective entrepreneurs are like mountain climbers because effective entrepreneurs know that the challenges they face, as an entrepreneur won't be easy. Some of these challenges include: getting financed, finding a market, having members of your team *jump ship,* dealing with bad attitudes, unexpected changes in the law, competition, and people telling you "NO" after "NO" after "NO." Yet, effective entrepreneurs hold firm and pursue their goal. Here are 8 Traits of Effective Entrepreneurs.

8 Traits of Effective Entrepreneurs

1. Failure is <u>not</u> the end!

An effective entrepreneur won't ever view failure as the end, but as an opportunity to learn, grow, mature, and sharpen their skills. They use their failures and setbacks as an opportunity to enhance their business skills and practices.

2. Stick to the plan but be flexible.

Effective entrepreneurs will also stick to their **business plan** but will make adjustments or shifts in it due to company growth or unexpected obstacles.

3. Being willing to learn.

Effective entrepreneurs are always willing to learn new information in order to be the best. Sometimes this involves taking a class, learning new software, or buying a book. Effective entrepreneurs do not run from learning but embrace it. They realize that if they allow themselves to fall behind in what is current, they will be left behind in the marketplace.

4. Focus on what you know, not what you don't know.

Effective entrepreneurs won't go around broadcasting their *Achilles* heel (weakness), but they will cleverly focus on the techniques that they know and/or familiar with to achieve their goal. As for their weakness, they will also build a team that embraces it as its strength.

5. Don't try to please everyone.

Effective entrepreneurs realize that they are different and that the people around them might not have the same aspirations nor understand their decisions. In spite of this, effective entrepreneurs remain confident, they never belittle their ideas to fit in, and realize they will never be accepted by everyone.

6. Being Resolute.

Effective entrepreneurs do not allow the fear of what people (or media, contemporaries, statistics, etc.) will say to sway their business convictions. Instead, they realize that there will always be people that doubt their decisions, the value of their product, or their ability to recover from financial disasters or failures. However, they ignore the negativity and move forward in success.

7. Embrace their Experiences.

Effective Entrepreneurs know that even if they don't have the experience, they will learn or find someone that can help them. Effective entrepreneurs do not allow fear of not having enough experience stop them from pursuing their goals. They realize that they will never know everything, but it's okay. In addition, they will not allow society limitations such as being "too young" or "too old" or "not having a college degree" or "not going to a top school" or "being of a certain gender or race" or any other boundaries to serve as a crutch in stopping them from trying.

8. Don't let money stop them from trying.

Effective entrepreneur realize that spending a little time praying, thinking creatively, and relying on your X-Factors will always help them find a way around the obstacle of money. They don't let the lack of financial resources stop them. Instead, they continue planning and moving forward while seeking out creative opportunities to meet their financial needs and expectations (i.e., raising funds through a garage sale, cashing in a forgotten savings bond, borrowing from a relative, bartering goods for services, buying what they need *used* as opposed to *new*, bargain shopping online for a deal, and others).

All of these traits will propel an entrepreneur into an effective entrepreneur and closer to the peak of achieving his/her goal. I pray that this chapter from me has been able to be a blessing unto you.

A Conversation with the Author: SBA = Advantage

SBA = Advantage refers to all the business resources that are *freely* available to you through your local United States Small Business Administration (SBA). The SBA has offices located throughout the United States of America to help people like you to be successful in business. Please visit them to find out what advantages they may have in store for you. The SBA's website is: www.SBA.gov. I pray that this insight from me has been able to be a blessing unto you.

Chapter XVII

Writing the Vision & Making it Plain

Writing the Vision & Making it Plain

"Goals that are not written down are just wishes."

Anonymous

Learning to "write your name" is one of the earliest lessons that we are taught in school. This small step is one of the most powerful hallmarks of entrepreneurship. Just like learning to write our name helped us to learn who we are, this valuable lesson fast-forwarded years in the future allows us to define our business through entrepreneurship. By having the faith to write your company's name as the first part of your business plan; you are on your way to writing the vision and making it plain.

What is the first step in writing the vision?

The first step is naming your business. Please name it here.

_ _

COMPANY NAME HERE

How can I make it Plain?

You make it plain by writing a business plan that is clear and simple. This makes your business plan easily understood, direct, and to the point. Some of the major components to be featured in your business plan may include your mission statement, services and/or goods, market, and other aspects of your business.

Below are some questions that will help you to write the components of your business plan. Remember, to keep your answers clear and simple. Here are 10 Strategic Questions to help you to craft a business plan. Please try answering the following questions:

10 Strategic Questions to Help You Craft a Business Plan

Question#1: What is the mission of your company?

In a business plan, the mission of a company is very important because it successfully articulates 1) the purpose in which the company was founded and 2) the goal(s) of the company. It is also one of the key components of any business plan as it is usually the first portion of a business plan that clients or investors will usually read. Here are two sample mission statements:

Sample A:
"The mission of Green Light Books & Publishing is to serve as an easy, effective, and user-friendly approach to Christian Authorship that will be published and distributed to all audiences. The ultimate goal of the company is become a dominant force in the Christian publishing industry."

Sample B:
"The mission of *ABC's Online Music Studio* is to feature a multitude of songs from musical artists and venues from around the world. The ultimate goal of the company is to serve the world as the premiere online music provider that will entertain all audiences that enjoy music."

Question#2: What services and/or goods will your business provide?

Goods are the products that your company provides. Services are duties your company performs. Both will earn revenue for your company. Some examples of goods and services are included below:

Goods
T-Shirts, Caps, Hair Products, Drinks, Books, Computers.

Services

Graphic Designer, Hair Stylist, Counseling, Consulting, Web-Design, Bookkeeping, Tutoring

Question#3: Who is the intended audience that your business will solicit its goods and/or services to?

Try to be as specific as possible because your audience is the intended market that you would like to have your goods and/or services reach. Some examples of audiences are included below:

<u>Audiences</u>
Young People (25 and under), Single women with children, Married couples under 30, Churches, high school students, people living in Florida, people that like dogs.

Question#4: Do you know at least 100 people (or businesses) that will benefit from your business?

If so, then list them on a separate sheet of paper. This group of 100 people will become the first people that will benefit from your business. Please include the name of each person or business and their contact information. Once your business has started, contact them to become your first business clients.

Question#5: How much can you afford to put towards this business venture?

By listing how much you can afford to reasonably put towards this business venture, you are articulating your start-up budget. Be sure to use the *Investitude Budget Worksheet* in Chapter 5 to find out if you can free up more money to use.

Now take that amount and research the industry online or at a local library and get books that will give you details on what your business entails (i.e., "How to Start a Restaurant," "How to Open a Clothing Line", etc.). If your business has never been done before, try to find a book with an industry that is as similar as possible and go from there.

Question#6: Are there any resources that you already have available (i.e. computer, etc?)

List all of the resources that you have available that you could possibly use toward making your idea a reality. This will become your start-up capital and/or equipment in getting your business going.

Question#7: Do you need other venues to raise additional funds for your business?

If yes, here are some potential venues that you can rely on and use to secure your business. Some of these areas may be in the form of a personal loan from yourself (or a family member) to your business, selling items that you no longer use at a garage sale to generate income, cashing in old savings bonds and/or other investments, hosting a fundraising dinner at your home, throwing a **launch party** at your home to earn additional money, scaling down your lifestyle so that you can save more of your income for a temporary amount of time, and/or taking out a loan from your 401k (Read: *Conversation with the Author in Chapter 21 for more information on 401k's*).

Question #8: Are there any people or other items that you need to build your business? If so, list them and their position and how they can help you.

By listing the people and job positions that you will need to make your business operate, you are identifying key areas that will make your business successful. One key suggestion is to think in terms of synergy and whom you can use to operate your business. Please see Chapter 13 for more information on synergy and finding people that can enhance your business. Also, here is an example:

Nature of Business: Publishing

<u>People Needed ~ Solution</u>	
Web-Designer	Hired college student to design website
Accountant	Purchased Accounting Software for less than $50.00

Question #9: Do you have a domain name?

If no, do you at least have an idea towards what would like your domain name to be? In this day and time, everyone needs some form of a website in order to be productive. If you are interested in an area to purchase your website, please visit: www.Investitude.com.

Question #10: What type of business structure would you like to use?

Please research various types of business structures and/or contact a local attorney in your state that can help you to determine the best business structure for your business.

* * *

Now that you have answered the aforementioned questions, use them to establish the foundation of your business plan. Let's immediately put your responses into action by turning them into business format by adhering to the following layout on the next page:

BUSINESS PLAN FOR

Corporate Name:

The name of my company is....

Mission Statement:

The mission is to....

The ultimate goal of the company is to...

Marketing Plan:

The products and/or services to be offered and sold will include:

Customer Base:

A profile of the intended customer base includes...

Organizational Structure:

(insert company name) will (or is) filed as a (insert type of business structure) under the State of (insert name of state) Law.

Present and Future Sources Of Capital:

Name	Amount	Cash or Assets	Date
Juan P. Chisholm	$10,000.00	Cash	Oct. 11

Technology to be Employed:

The technology that will be employed to facilitate the business activities will include a website.

* * *

Great job! I hope this layout helps you in getting started in writing your vision and making it plain.

Is there anything else I should know?

Now that you have a foundation for your business plan, find a business attorney in your area that can help you in selecting a legal structure, filing formation documents, applying for licenses, and complying with federal and state requirements. The attorney may also be able to help you in legally protecting your ideas (filing for a copyrights, trademarks, or patents, etc).

Extra Money Saving Tip

If you cannot afford a lawyer initially, try contacting your local law school. Most law schools offer law clinics that allow graduating law students to work on your business with the supervision of practicing attorneys. This service is generally **free** for members of the community that qualify based on their financial need.

I pray that this chapter from me has been able to be a blessing unto you.

A Conversation with the Author:

Need Help with Business Structure & Formation

As a law student at the Florida A&M University College of Law, I have learned something very interesting about most law schools and students. Most law schools have a business law section where they offer services to the community by establishing businesses free of charge. In turn, law students gain valuable on the job training that gives them real interaction with clients. There are of course drawbacks to taking advantage of this community service. The knowledge of the students is typically limited and it often takes them at least an academic semester to complete services for clients since it is in conjunction with their class schedule.

Alternatively, I recommend finding a business law attorney and/or a financial firm that has expertise in small business finance to help you establish your business. There are a number of technical considerations that you can implement in the beginning stages of your enterprise that will save you time, money, and headaches in the future. These professionals offer a bevy of knowledge that can help position you for growth and success in the future. Both of these venues should provide you with assistance in selecting your business structure and/or formation. I pray that this chapter from me has been able to be a blessing unto you.

Chapter XVIII

Expert Status

Expert Status

"A Fish Can Only Grow To The Size of Its Bowl."
Traditional Saying

Experts are paid more for their specialized knowledge and proficiency in a selected field. Once the *buzz* is out that you are **competent** at what you do and that you possess specialized knowledge in some given field, you could in fact become known as an expert. This can be a real advantage especially if you are an entrepreneur because potential clients will 1) seek you out for your expert knowledge, reputation, and insight and 2) it will likely increase your client base and professional portfolio as an entrepreneur. If you are competent and possess proficiency and specialized knowledge in a given area, here are 9 ways that you can promote your Expert Status.

9 Effective Ways to Promote Your Expert Status

1. Make business cards and give them to people you encounter making them aware of your skills and the services you provide (i.e., in stores, at work, at school, at family reunions, people at church, etc.)

2. Encourage and allow your friends and/or past clients to talk about you. It's okay to allow them to rave about you as it will increase business and spread the word that you are good (or bad).

3. Make a press release and distribute it to various media outlets (i.e., radio stations, television networks, community newsletters, internet blogs, newspapers).

4. Start an email newsletter and occasionally send it to your network of supporters keeping them updated on your recent developments in your field of expertise.

5. Accept local speaking engagements related to your specialized area. This will help you establish yourself and become known as an authority on that particular topic.

6. Volunteer and write a column in the local newspapers, magazines, or community newsletters. This of course could attract some huge attention for you and your business. It will allow you to be seen by the public as an expert. In turn, it could put your name, work ethic, and reputation in the public eye for scrutiny. Be mindful of this, but don't allow it to prevent you from going forward.

7. Get connected in your community. This can be achieved by joining a local church, community or

civic organization, hobby group, or book club. This will help you in promoting your Expert Status.

8. Attend conferences related to fields that are associated with your industry. Go where people are looking for individuals with your expertise. For example, if you have expertise in providing marketing tips, go to a business conference where business owners are present that would need the services you provide. There, the solicitation of your services (in the form of business cards, presentations, or networking) would be greatly appreciated.

9. Write a book. Consider using your experiences and credentials to publish your own book based on your expertise. Being an author is a great way to establish yourself in your field as well as generate income to pursue your projects.

A Conversation with the Author:

Doing Business As 'D.B.A' Dirt

In popular culture or what is often dictated by the television, movies, and/or media outlets, it's easy to *think* that intentionally conducting in fraudulent and/ or other corrupt behavior such as cheating, deceiving, misleading, and doing dirt to people, clients, and other businesses is the only way to make it *big* in business. But I disagree and I think you should as well. Because by partaking in intentional deceptive means to make money, not only are you condoning unethical business practices that are unacceptable, you are harming yourself, your reputation, your family, and others that are connected to your business. It is also this type of selfish negative nature that makes people untrusting of business and could in fact, cost you to be placed in jail. Is intentionally partaking in fraudulent or other corrupt behavior really worth taking the chance of earning a hefty fine or prison sentence? I don't think so.

But what I do believe is that we, as business owners, entrepreneurs, investors, experts, and others have an obligation to conduct ourselves in an ethical manner that will restore trust back in our market and promote fair dealing and good will for others and ourselves. Every successful person knows that it's easy to intentionally do the wrong thing. But it takes true strength, integrity, character, and discipline to recognize that something is wrong and that you can get away with it, but still chooses to make the right choice in our money-driven society. Make it your priority to not engage in crooked business practices and be a credit to society (not another charlatan). I pray that this insight from me has been able to be a blessing unto you.

UNIT FIVE: INVESTING

Chapter XIX

THINK LIKE AN INVESTOR

Think Like An Investor

"Anyone who thinks the sky is the limit, has limited imagination."

Anonymous

Thinking like an investor requires three powerfully charged components: envisioning your success; having a winning spirit in spite of your failures; and not being moved by material possessions, but the end goal—your future financial success.

One of the most powerful venues that you are able to control is your mind. If you can learn to guard it and protect (or monitor) what goes inside of it by only allowing positive thoughts and beliefs to enter, you will ignite the motor in your mind to *"greatness."* This will allow you to envision what your life would be like if you had a solid financial future and/or retirement already established. What starts with a notion, like, "You can do it," then, becomes a real thought that you believe in. Believing that you can do something will eventually translate into you visualizing your goal being accomplished. And, if I can challenge you to take hold of that abstract faith in front of you, believing that there is more out there for you, you will have opened up an even bigger and brighter door in your life that will guide you towards your future financial success. Envisioning your success is a powerful component to thinking like an investor.

In addition, thinking like an investor is also realizing that people that invest will eventually make mistakes and errors with their finances. But when these mistakes occur, investors also realize that falling to these negative hurdles is not terminal despite how painful they feel or how bad things may look. Instead, thinking like an investor allows the investor "to get up" and "move on" as a winner by continuing to be able, willing, and ready in pursuit of reaching their investment goals. Having this type of winning attitude in spite of what happens also translates into other successes for the investor. Moreover, this type of can do spirit also means that you won't allow yourself to adopt negative and life-staggering mindsets. These mindsets say that you either can't or won't be successful in finance or investing (or any other areas of your life) simply because of where you were born, what you look like, the community you grew up in, where your parents worked, how much you currently have, past mistakes or failures, and any other negative hurdles that will prevent you from being motivated to win. So be positive by seeing yourself able, willing, and ready to compete! This type of confidence will trigger you to the level of greatness that you desire and open up your life to operate at the destined place in which you were meant to be—thinking like an investor.

Lastly, thinking like an investor means you are not moved by ideas of just having material possessions (i.e., like cars, shoes, fancy clothes) right now. But, your priority is working towards the end goal. Admittedly, being able to see the end goal before material possessions is not always easy, but it can be done. Especially, if you can learn to view your *true wealth* as not being predicated on material possessions, but in seeing yourself as God's best creation and through Him, you are whole and complete in spite of what you have or don't have. Moreover, try appreciating and reflecting on the things that you were already fortunate enough to have. Also, thinking of how your sacrifice now will bless you, your family, others, and generations here and in the future all as a result of you working toward the end goal will also keep you focused on your true wealth.

Moreover, in thinking like an Investor, you have to envision yourself as becoming successful. Next, you must be willing to maintain a positive outlook in spite of your failures. Lastly, you can't allow your decisions to be based on material possessions now, but on focusing on the end goal. These powerful components contribute to thinking like an investor and will positively contribute to you achieving your investment goals.

Through the course of this unit, I will be discussing various investment venues that will help you to have the right Investitude in reference to your investments and investment decisions. Areas to be discussed will include: IRAs & 401Ks, high yield savings accounts, prepaid college programs, home ownership, and pulling your credit report. Please feel free to research companies that offer these specific investment venues and other outside information to make an informed investment decision.

Are Investments Always Safe?

Generally speaking, the answer to this question is largely dependant upon the type of investment. Although as a rule of thumb, the greater the return on the investment, the more risk is involved with that particular investment. In other words, the more you could earn from a particular investment, the more likely of a risk it presents to you to lose money. For a detailed explanation of the various risks associated with investments, please reference my first book: How to Make Your Past, A Blessing to Your Future (ISBN: 0-9755110-0-9).

Are there any secrets that investors rely on to make money?

Yes, having the latest and most up-to-date information is the key! The reason that some people feel that investors or investing is so beyond them is because they feel that they do not possess enough knowledge. Don't allow this to become your crutch. There are several investment books and various investment newspapers and magazines that you can subscribe to that are bound to give you sufficient information to allow you to make informed financial decisions.

Also, investors are usually cognizant of the following factors: **Time, Financial Discipline, and Consistency** and how these factors affect one's finances and their financial decisions.

What is so important about Time, Discipline, and Consistency?

Time

Time is important for the following three reasons:

1. *Time allows you to grow your money.*

This means that the more time you have to grow your money (invest it in something and leave it alone), the more money that you will make from your investments. For example, based off of the element of time alone, a person that starts to invest in a reputable investment in their twenties that relies on **compounding interest** will have earned more than a person that started to invest in their thirties. Alternatively, a person that started to invest in their thirties will have earned more than a person that started to invest in the forties. Thus, the more time that you have to invest your money; the more potential that it has to grow and earn you additional dollars.

2. *Having time gives more room for error.*

This means that when you decide to invest early, you have more time to make mistakes. Moreover, mistakes for a younger investor, could teach them an important life lesson to make them an even savvier investor. Plus, they still have years in the workforce to earn more money to replace that which they may have lost and start over. But a mistake made by an older investor could be so costly that the person could end up forfeiting their entire life savings or retirement funds without the means of replenishing it. Again, start investing as early as possible to avoid these types of mistakes.

3. ***Time allows you to be more strategic with your investment decisions.***

This means that the more time you have, the more options or strategies you have at your disposal. Investors usually determine what is in their best interests based off of factors such as (1) age and (2) the person's **level of risk**.

Discipline

In order to be disciplined, you must have "SAG."

S—Strength to resist the temptation to spend.

A—Accountability to yourself and your finances to make decisions to do what's in the best interest of your finances and financial future (i.e. budgeting, sacrificing, saving, investing, etc.)

G—Goal Setting will provide you with a plan to set goals towards your financial success with your future in mind.

Discipline = Strength + Accountability + Goal Setting

Consistency

Consistency—Being *committed* to the end goal.

Finally, investors know the importance of consistency. This allows you to be committed to putting the same or greater amount of money aside each month in order to invest it towards the end goal. However, one point of clarification, putting money aside to be invested does not mean that each month you have to put the same amount in the same investment. Thusly, be wise in your investment decisions. If you personally feel that one of your investments is not bearing the particular fruit that you would like to taste, then it's okay to put it in another one of your investments or just wait. The goal is for your money to be working hard for you by earning more while invested. Various investment products fluctuate based on the market so it is alright to adjust your strategy accordingly (e.g., moving your funds from a risky stock to a consistent interest bearing money market account).

Alternatively, consistency as described here, could be just earmarking your proceeds to invest it on a later date. Also, please note that you may encounter some unexpected events that may cause you to start over (e.g., losing a job, family illness, etc.). These types of unfortunate hurdles should be expected. However, as you go through it, remember to **have a winning spirit in spite of what is happening** and be willing to get back up and start over towards your goal.

What If I <u>don't</u> have the money to invest or be a consistent investor?

One solution is to use the *Investitude Budgeting Worksheet* found in Chapter 5 to free up at least $100.00 per month (or as close to it as possible). Try to use this money to start investing or to be a consistent investor.

Is There Anything Else I Should Know?

Yes, there are several investment scams. Here are three suggestions to avoid them.

Firstly, always research companies and various investments prior to putting your money in them. You can type their names in a search engine on the Internet to read newspaper articles relating to their business practices and overall reputation. You may also ask friends and relatives for recommendations of investment companies. However, make sure that you ask reputable contacts that have made sound financial decisions themselves.

Secondly, avoid investments that you hear about via email, mail, and/or phone calls by companies that you have never heard of. They could be potential scams. Stay away from them!

Thirdly, always ask about hidden fees and costs associated with the investment product. The last thing you want is to invest your hard earned money only to watch it be devoured by hidden costs.

10 Final Steps that will Help you to Think More Like an Investor!

1. The earlier you invest, the better off you will be.
2. Educate yourself. Never invest in something that you don't understand completely.
3. Exercise discipline in your investment decisions.
4. Be consistent, but pay attention to the market to make sure you are investing in the right thing at the right time.
5. Avoid scams!

6. Set investment goals.
7. Before throwing money into an investment, make sure that you have researched the company and the products they are offering.
8. Discipline yourself to be consistent with your investments.
9. Start setting short-terms and long-term goals with your money.
10. To avoid worrying, don't check on your investments too frequently.

I pray that this insight from me has been able to be a blessing unto you.

A Conversation with the Author:

Investment Reflections

When you start to think like an Investor, you start to realize that investing is not about the person having the most money to invest or the biggest pockets to pool money from. But instead, you start to realize that investing is often times about making simple, strategic, small, financial decisions *at the right time* and *in the right investment vehicle* to positively impact your financial future and life. My first book: How to Make Your Past, A Blessing to Your Future [ISBN: 0-9755110-0-9] was designed to reveal this to its readers by embracing the simple yet crucial element of time to make investment decisions. In addition, it engages readers in an in-depth exploration of various investment vehicles including: stocks, bonds, mutual funds, certificates of deposits, investment clubs, wills, and others in order to help readers to make important, solid, financial decisions. It not only explains each investment in great detail but answers frequently asked questions and includes investment strategies and actual plans of action for how to use each one to your financial advantage.

As a result, the insight from How to Make Your Past, A Blessing To Your Future will **not** be duplicated in this unit or any other area in Investitude. Please purchase a copy of it if you would like to explore those topics in more detail. For more information, please visit: www.JuanChisholm.com. I pray that this insight from me has been able to be a blessing unto you.

Chapter XVIII

Home Ownership

Home Ownership

There is an elite club in America that affords its members such privileges as tax breaks and increased net worth through effortless appreciation. It also serves as a place of protection where its members can seek refuge and safety from outside forces. In addition, it is a place of liberty, where its members are free to pursue their dreams, operate their dreams, and live their dreams. Lastly, it is a place where monthly dues are lower (in comparison to making rent payments for non-club members) that can oftentimes be set around it's members personal budget. So, how can I join this elite club? You can join by owning or purchasing a home.

How Can Having A Home Increase My Net Worth?

Having a home can (1) increase your *net value* and (2) bring in revenue.

1. Having a home increases your net value because the market value of the house is added to the value of your other personal assets (e.g., car, jewelry, cash in the bank).

2. Also, having a home could add to your residual income as an investment if you choose to rent it

out to a tenant. If you do choose to rent it out, please be sure that your rent is higher than the mortgage and to gradually increase the rent between 2%-6% each year based on the surrounding market. Also please note that you may have to increase the rent by a higher amount if the insurance or taxes associated with the property increases. Please contact a real estate lawyer to draft a lease agreement and explain to you your duties and obligations as a landlord based on your state's law.

3 Factors that Discourage People from Purchasing a Home:

1. *"I can't afford to do it!"*

Sure, not having enough money is a valid reason to not purchase a home. But this is an easy hurdle to overcome. Moreover, with the amount of federal and private funding programs available at your disposal, you can overcome this hurdle of not having enough money by finding a funding program that will work with you. Some available home ownership programs in your community can be contacted by doing the following:

❖ Contacting your local bank or credit union.

- ❖ Researching home ownership programs via books from your local library, the phonebook, or the Internet.

- ❖ Asking a friend or a family member what they did or who they spoke with in order to get their home.

All of these serve as valuable sources of information that will help you to get over the syndrome of thinking that you can't afford a home and walk into your dream of home ownership.

2. **It's Too Complicated!**

Buying a home is just as complicated as renting an apartment. The same elements apply; just different terminology (e.g., lease v. mortgage). Don't allow this to stop you from owning your home! Pick up a book from your local bookstore or library and educate yourself on the process. You will find out that buying a home is just like renting an apartment, but at the end of the paperwork, you are the owner (not the renter).

3. **I'm Scared!**

Fear is not a reason but an excuse and a dangerous weapon to be used against you. If you are afraid to purchase a home, then your fear could be causing you to miss out on one of the best decisions of your life. Do not allow fear to hold you hostage, but break away from it and purchase your home as your new place of refuge.

Don't let these 3 Factors discourage you from purchasing your home! Join the club by becoming the homeowner that you would like to be.

How can I reduce fees?

One of the most well informed people when it comes to reducing your payment is **not the person selling the home**, but the person sitting in front of you that is responsible for doing your paperwork (i.e., the loan processor, bank officer, etc). It's always important to ask this person "Are there any grants or special programs that I may be able to qualify for?" The answer may vary from "No" to "it depends on various factors such as your current job, schooling, number of people in your household, spouse, first-time home owner, and others." If you qualify for one of these programs, it could save you tons of cost.

However, my only caution is that you carefully read through the paperwork and have them to explain the terminology in the agreement or have an attorney look over the agreement. There may also be local agencies in your area that can explain your mortgage paperwork. Please consult them for more information if you need further assistance in understanding your individual mortgage paperwork, the grant, and/or special program that you are trying to qualify.

Also, an important rule of thumb: **If the person doesn't know the answer(s) to your questions or is seemingly trying to avoid your questions, then this person may not be the person or business that you need to deal with.** An evasive answer or an "I don't know" to an important question now may cost you hundreds of dollars in regrets later. So, if the person or business can't answer your important questions, find someone else or another company.

What are questions I should ask before closing on my home?

A company may try to be evasive about any of the following questions:

- "Is this a sub-prime loan?"

Sub-prime loans and predatory lending practices are the types of practices that have contributed to the demise of the real estate market. Avoid these loans at all cost! They are dangerous because this type of loan could in fact lead to a foreclosure. If the person admits that you are being offered one of the following loans or they are unsure, **please walk away and leave this company or person alone!** There are millions of other available opportunities and programs that will work better to serve your real estate interest. Sub-prime loans could be offered through mortgage brokers, banks, and loan officers. Be careful and avoid sub-prime loans!

- "Is this an adjustable rate loan?"

Adjustable rates are unpredictable rates that vary depending on various factors outside of your control. These are not the types of loans that you want to get stuck in for the next 10, 15, 20, or 30 years because they are unpredictable. When you have an adjustable rate mortgage, the amount you pay varies from a random percentage (like 6.57%) to a higher percentage (17.14%) or a lower one (6.19%). These types of periodical changes will remain through the life of your loan. **This is not what you want!** Instead, you want to demand a **fixed interest rate**. This will ensure that your rate is the same for the life of the loan no matter what.

What If I Already Have a Home? Is there any way to reduce my payments?

Sure, if you have a home, here are 3 solutions to help you to reduce your payments.

3 Solutions to Help You Reduce Your Current Mortgage Payments.

SOLUTION #1: Remove *PMI* with 20%

If you already have a home and you would like to reduce your payments, solution # 1 is to attack the PMI payments added to your mortgage. *PMI* stands for ***Private Mortgage Insurance,*** which is traditionally associated with paying on a mortgage to further ensure that your lenders are paid. Moreover, it is traditionally associated with mortgage loans that may have been paid for by a 100% loan or in any loan in which you may have put down less than 20% of the purchase price as your down payment. As a result, you have PMI payments. However, once 20% of your mortgage is paid, you can have your PMI payments removed by simply calling your lender and asking the lender to remove the PMI payments. By removing PMI, you can reduce your monthly mortgage payments. Be sure to have them to mail you a confirmation in writing to formally confirm that PMI was removed and for your personal records. Also, if you find out that you have been paying PMI and it should have been removed prior to you asking for it to be removed, you want to demand that the overage you paid to the company be returned to you in the form of a check.

Solution# 2: Remove PMI with Increases in Property Value

Sometimes people don't have the money to cover PMI. A second solution may be for you to rely on appreciation (increasing property values). In other words, if your property value has increased, this may contribute to your PMI payments being reduced because the higher property value will allow you to reach the 20% much faster. Contact your mortgage company to see if they will be willing to reduce your PMI payments in lieu of your increasing property value. If they agree, be sure to have them to mail you a confirmation in writing to formerly confirm that PMI was removed and for your personal records.

SOLUTION # 3: Add Extra Money to Your Mortgage

Make additional small, yet meaningful payments toward your mortgage balance. As you become more comfortable doing this, you can gradually increase the amount, which will chip more away from your mortgage balance. For example, after each payment you can either tack on an additional amount toward the principal (not the interest) of your mortgage and over time, gradually increase it. Ultimately, this will reduce your balance and allow you to repay your mortgage faster. Please contact your lender to make sure that you are not penalized for paying off your mortgage early.

I pray that this chapter from me has been able to be a blessing unto you.

A Conversation with the Author:

Tired of Receiving Junk Credit Card Mail?

What's in your mail? I am guessing that the same thing that is in mine—an over abundance of annoying credit card, insurance, and other information with all my personal information on it. This type of mail is not innocent because once you receive it, if you do not completely shred it up, it could lead to someone getting your precious information and stealing your identify (i.e., identity theft). But, there is a solution to this annoying mail madness and the great news is that it only takes less than 2 minutes to complete to stop you from receiving the mail madness and other mail solicitation for 5 years. It's simple. All you do is call the following number and by doing so, you are choosing to stop receiving the thousands of offers from credit cards and other companies. Here's the number: **1-888-567-8688.** Enjoy!

Now that I have done it, I'm excited about opening the mailbox and *not* receiving tons of solicitations. I pray that this chapter from me has been able to be a blessing unto you.

Chapter XXI

Having A Million Dollars In the Palm of Your Hand—IRA's

Having A Million Dollars in the Palm of Your Hand –IRA's

"The tragedy of life is not that it ends so soon, but that we wait so long to begin it."

Anonymous

My wife and I started our first IRA in our twenties.

Do you play the lottery? In America, millions of people play the lotto everyday in hopes of winning millions and millions of dollars. But mathematically speaking, what are the chances of any of those millions of people winning millions of dollars from the lottery? The answer to this question is that the chances of one of those millions of people winning the lottery jackpot only exists in an imaginary reality (not the real one that we live in). This means that statistically, if one million people played the lottery each day in hopes of winning millions and millions of dollars, not even one of them is likely to ever win. This makes perfect sense if you are in the lottery business. So, instead of relying on the lottery as a million dollar solution, here's a real way to earn a million dollars—**IRA's.** IRAs make obtaining a million dollars closer to your reach than you could have ever imagined.

What is an IRA?

Generally speaking, there are many different types of IRAs. Depending on the type that you select, it provides either a tax-free or a tax-deferred way of saving for retirement. IRAs rely on **compound interest** to grow your retirement funds at exponential rates. The government has been steadily increasing the maximum contribution, which should make these retirement vehicles an even more attractive investment option. Funds can usually be withdrawn without penalty at age 59 and ½.

How can an IRA earn you a million dollars?

Because IRA's rely on compound interest, they can cause your money to grow in amazing ways. This especially becomes beneficial when you consider the following factors: (1) age, (2) how early your start making your contributions, and (3) the amount of money you are willing to put towards the IRA each year. Through IRA's, these combined factors could help you to earn a million dollars in retirement.

In other words, the earlier you start to contribute to an IRA, the better off you will be in your retirement.

How can my money growing at an exponential rate benefit me?

First, it gives you more *bang for your buck.* In other words, compound interest allows your money to grow more quickly and rapidly instead of at a steady gradual rate. This is a very effective way to grow your retirement resources if you are in a position of investing for the long term.

How can I get an IRA for myself or my family?

It's easy. If you would like to get an IRA for you or a member of your family, all you have to do is contact your local bank, credit union, or brokerage firm. Please note that IRA rates may vary depending on the type of business that you select. For more information about IRAs, please visit www.Investitude.com or contact your local financial service provider.

3 Ways to Exponentially Grow Your IRA Earnings.

1. Start investing in an IRA as soon as possible!

2. Stay consistent with your IRA investment by contributing the maximum allowable amount or by gradually increasing the amount you contribute each year.

3. Carefully research the tax benefits and limitations associated with each type of IRA. Alternatively, please consult a tax specialist to further explain how having an IRA will affect your taxes or the person that it is being purchased for.

* * *

I pray that this insight from me has been able to be a blessing unto you.

A Conversation with the Author:

Free Money for 401k Users

Looking for a goldmine?

Try looking through your employer sponsored 401K plan. If your employer offers one, then this may be the retirement vehicle that you have been looking for to chisel your retirement funds into. 401Ks allow you to put your funds aside at least until you are 59 ½ to be used towards your retirement.

Now, what makes a 401K a goldmine? 4 Major reasons: Firstly, many employers offering 401Ks have matching programs that will match employee contributions up to a certain percentage or dollar for dollar. That means the company itself is giving you free money toward your retirement in addition to your own contributions. Secondly, if you are contemplating starting a business or other important project that you don't have the immediate capital to use, you can oftentimes tap into these accounts and take a loan on your 401K instead of relying on the bank. This will work wonders because instead of worrying about paying the bank back, you are paying yourself back - which is not as stressful especially considering the fact that your personal collateral is not up for grabs as it would be if you went though the bank (i.e., your home, car, etc.). Thirdly, it's easy to roll over if you leave your employer and go to a new company. Rolling over allows you to put it in a new company's 401k plan or roll it over to a new account. Lastly, in cases of an emergency, 401k's often times offer hardship withdrawals which will allow you to withdraw funds from your 401K (subjecting you to taxes and a 10% penalty) when you are facing severe financial hardship or an emergency. Other hardship withdrawals include: purchasing a home, paying for education, to prevent home eviction or foreclosure, or other forms of extreme financial hardship. Although you subject yourself to financial penalty and hardship, this could come in handy if you have a 401K, but you are in a very tough financial position. Hardship withdrawals should be a last resort. Please consult your 401K plan administrator before relying on these major reasons. So next time you think of a goldmine, think of your 401K and get to chiseling. I pray that this chapter from me has been able to be a blessing unto you.

Chapter XXII

High Yield Savings Accounts

High Yield Savings Accounts: An Alternative Banking Option

"Winning is not just about taking chances. It's about having a good attitude despite the outcome."
Juan Phillip Chisholm

Who would you want to win today? There is an age-old debate between the tortoise and the hare and which character should have really won that race? Some people side with the tortoise for it's slow yet steady pace that wins the race. Others tend to side with the hare for its speed and obvious potential to physically outrun the tortoise. Just like in this depiction, when it comes to your money, whom would you prefer? Would it be the slow and steady low-interest saving account as provided through the bank. Or, would you prefer the fast, higher yielding saving account as provided through an online bank. Assuming that the Federal Deposit Insurance Corporation (FDIC), which usually insures an account up to a certain amount, equally insures both the bank and online bank which one would you prefer?

What are some of the major factors that distinguish these accounts?

Some of the major factors that distinguish these accounts include: interest rates, access, safety, and security. Let me explain.

Higher Interest Rates:

Higher interest rates tend to keep high yield savings accounts competitive when compared to brick and mortar banks and credit unions. Interest rates for these saving accounts usually range between 2%-5% on average. Because high yield saving accounts are managed through online banks, they do not have the business overhead that traditional banks have and they are able to offer higher interest rates to their customers. If having higher interest is your only banking concern, you may want to consider having a high yield savings accounts. For a list of online high-yielding saving accounts, please visit: www.Investitude.com.

Access To Your Money:

Having access to your money is a major concern for everyone. Local banks allow you to withdraw and deposit your money with ease (usually within 24 hours by entering and exiting your bank during its hours of operations. If having immediate access to your money is your top banking concern, you may be more comfortable leaving your money in a local bank or credit union.

However, if you do not mind waiting between 3 to 7 days to receive money withdrawn (or transferred) from your high-yield saving account, then online banking may be the ideal situation for you. Both accounts will likely provide you with the feature of viewing your money 24 hours a day, 7 days a week via your computer, online service provider, or other electronic device.

Safety and Security:

As long as the brick and mortar bank and the online bank are FDIC Insured, your money should be safe up to the amount it is FDIC insured. However, please note that just because your money is FDIC insured, this does not mean that you can become careless with your financial information by carelessly leaving around bank receipts with your account number on it; or web browsers open with your bank account information available; or leave passwords saved on a public computer. Please take precautions by guarding and securing all your financial information.

* * *

Fortunately, in light of the aforementioned factors of interest rates, access, safety, and security, it's really up to you and what you feel more comfortable with. Please choose whatever works best for you! Alternatively, if you cannot decide, you can always choose both. I pray that this insight from me has been able to be a blessing unto you.

A Conversation with the Author:

Online Banking versus Local Banks

In reality, the debate between high yield savings accounts managed through online banking and local banks is really a tale of two cities that both need each other in order to co-exist. In my opinion, online banks keep local banks fair with their interest rates, while local banks serve as a means for online banks to work in conjunction with them to deposit funds. I opened up my first major brick and mortar bank account at age fourteen. I opened up my first online bank account when I was about twenty-four years old. To this day, I still use both of them. It just depends on what's going on to determine which one really gets my dollars.

For example, short-term financial tasks (i.e., dealing with immediate cash on hand, receiving paychecks, personal compensations, financial gifts, and other forms of personal revenue) are usually deposited into my brick and mortar bank account. In addition, I use that same account to pay out bills (i.e., mortgage, car insurance, electricity, gas, etc.) and other expenses.

However, when I am trying to put money aside for future use and/or savings (i.e., save money for over a month, or earmark funds to invest in other projects on a later date, or towards a personal emergency fund), I always tend to safe keep these funds into a High-Yielding Savings Account. Having both of these accounts help me by keeping my finances separated. I pray that this chapter of my life has been able to be a blessing unto yours.

Chapter XXI

Planning for a College Education

Planning for a College Education

"An obstacle is something you see when you take your eyes off the goals you are trying to reach."

Anonymous

One of the most difficult tasks for people to plan towards is a college education.

As a teacher, I have learned that one of the main distinctions that determines who actually goes to college or not is not intellect, good grades, classroom etiquette, successes, awards, or accolades. Instead, the decision to go to college often comes down to who has the money and who does not. This reveals a sad commentary that stifles many good families and students alike and is a terrible reason for anyone to not pursue a college education. But instead of just focusing on the problem, here is just one solution to help you to get over the college financial hurdle—having a Pre-Paid College Plan. It is an effective way to finance your college aspirations or the aspirations of someone that you know.

What is A Pre-Paid College Plan?

Many states in America offer Pre-Paid College Plans for students that are interested in going to college in that particular state. Many of the programs also lock in rates for students at the time the program is started and if the student does not go to school in that particular state, many of the programs offer full refunds. They serve as a great way to lock in tuition rates and finance college aspirations early on.

What are the benefits?

Although benefits vary by state, some of the more common ones include:

1. You can lock in tuition rates.

2. Your child's college tuition is gradually paid for throughout your son or daughter's childhood, which means that the lump sum burden of paying for college doesn't fall on you on their high school graduation day.

3. If your child receives scholarships or doesn't go to school in that particular state, the programs will usually allow full refunds or may charge a minimal fee. Please consult your specific state for the answer to this question.

4. If your child does want to leave the state, some of the programs have transfer programs that will allow you to transfer your funds to other states in which they may be honored to offset some of the cost of tuition in another state.

How can I get one?

For starters, you can try visiting the website listed below that will provide you with further insight on prepaid college plans and link you to your state's prepaid college program(s). Please visit the following:

http://www.collegesavings.org

These sites offer numerous advantages to people trying to plan a college education from Pre-K level students up to high-school juniors or seniors. By carefully planning the right program, you will have strategically positioned yourself to effortlessly pay for the college education of your child. And because you planned for it, you will not feel the burden or hole in your pocket of paying for college at the last minute. These will also make great birthday gifts for children.

What If My Child Leaves the State to Pursue College?

Generally, it depends on the state that you live in. In some cases, you can either (1) transfer your funds to the other state's educational plan, or get your money back. But in other cases, you may be penalized by a fee and then able to get the remainder of your money back. Please contact the state's educational plan for more information by visiting the aforementioned website.

Next, try utilizing this website: www.fafsa.org. This is a great resource because it allows you to solicit the government for grants and/or work-study programs by filling out the Online Financial Aid application to help you to get ahead when it comes to planning for college. It is good to start completing the form on this website at the beginning of your child's junior or senior year in high school. One of the advantages of doing this early is that you get it out of the way. Some of the tools you will need include: IRS Tax Returns and other similar information.

Are there ways that I can set money aside towards this college plan?

Yes. Set a goal with the monthly amount that you would like to have each month towards your child's (or children's) college plan. Then, use the *Investitude Budgetting Worksheet* to free up any additional money and use it toward the college plan. Remember parents, a small sacrifice at age two, will bless your child (or children) to go to college at age 18. And they will also appreciate it!

Will these Prepaid Programs work for graduate students?

Typically, Yes. Please consult your specific state to find out more details about its program.

Do you know of other ways for graduate students to find money?

Yes. If you are interested in pursuing a graduate degree (i.e. an MBA, J.D., Masters in some field, Ph.D., LLM, etc.) usually graduate students not only have to deal with finding money, but also juggling time against real life issues. For a graduate level student, I suggest that you take the following 4 Tips:

4 Tips to Help Graduate Students Find Money

1. Check with your employer to find out if there are any programs that they may offer to help you pay for your school. (i.e., a program that covers up to 6 credit hours if you earn a "C" or better, etc.)

2. Check with your financial aid officer or loan processor for school specific scholarships at the university or institution you are applying for.

3. Find out the benefits of being a teaching assistant (TA) or graduate assistant. If your school offers TA's with either reduced or no tuition, this may be something that you may want to pursue.

However, be sure to carefully consider the workload and time commitment and make sure that you are able to balance your academic course load with other real life commitments.

4. Please read Chapter 13 on Scholarships.

I pray that you use this information wisely and that this insight from me has been able to be a blessing unto you.

Conversation with the Author:

"I know that credit cards are bad, but I am getting one anyway."

There are always some people that admit that they understand that credit cards are usually bad and yet, they choose to get it anyway. To any such group, I do not recommend getting a credit card. But I do recognize that for some, this may be the only option in cases of an emergency. Here's a conversation that may help you to make the right credit card decision. It features 8 solid suggestions to cover you and prevent you from making a terrible credit card decision. Here are 8 factors to thoroughly consider before signing up for a credit card for emergencies:

1. Read through your credit card material!!
2. Read through your credit card material despite how boring it may seem!!! Failure to do this can prove to be fatal to you and your finances. Please read through your credit card material and if you do not understand it, ask questions. If the person does not know the answers, then it is likely the wrong card for you!
3. Call their customer service number and assess how helpful they are. How long were you on hold? Were they very accessible or was it difficult to reach a person? How flexible are they with bill payments—must it be received

in the mail on the date of or will they accept payments via the phone or online? Are there any fees for payment? Yes, sometimes, credit companies charge you a fee to pay your bill if you are not paying it a certain way.

4. Only use it in cases of emergency
5. Try to get one with a low-interest rate with a fixed amount.
6. Always shop around for the lowest interest rate. I can guarantee you that if the rate is 28%, it's the wrong one. Also, please try to find one that offers interest at a range that you can count on your fingers (1-10%).
7. Please be mindful that even if your interest rate is alleged that it is fixed, credit cards usually have mandatory policies that increase interest rates in different seasons. For example, the rate for the fall and spring may be less than those associated with summer and winter. These rate shifts are usually associated with the shopping habits of consumers (i.e. usually people spend more over the summer because people tend to take vacations and students are out of school and in the winter months people usually celebrate Christmas and other holidays that usually cause people to travel and/or purchase gifts). Read through your credit card material to know when these rate shifts will affect you.
8. Pay your bill before interest begins to accrue.

I pray that this insight from me has been a blessing unto you.

Chapter XXIV

A Look in the Mirror: Pulling Your Credit Report

A Look in the Mirror: Pulling Your Credit Report

"An inventor fails 999 times, and if he succeeds once, he's in. He treats his failures simply as practice shots."

Anonymous

Even when I decided to look in the mirror and pull my own credit report for the first time, there were some things on it that just didn't belong. As a result, I responded.

Can the mirror lie? If it's your credit report, it surely can. If you are relying on your credit report as the sole indicator of your credit business reliability, or personal liabilities, you are making a mistake! It is a fallacy to believe that this important document is always truthful. And unfortunately, if the mirror reflection of a credit report will deceive you, it will also deceive others (i.e., prospective lenders, employers, business partners) about your reliability. So, in order to get the fairest credit report, maybe you should ask the famous question: "Mirror, Mirror, on the wall, how can I get the fairest credit report of them all?"

How Can I Get the Fairest Credit Report?

Here are 4 simple steps to help you 'see' the fairest credit report.

1st Contact www.AnnualCreditReports.com to get a free credit report for a limited time or pay one of the credit companies listed below to see your report and score.

Credit Agency	**Website Address**
Trans Union Credit	www.truecredit.com
Equifax, Inc.	www.equifax.com/

2nd: Thoroughly look over the report and write down anything that you think may be wrong or is questionable.

3rd: Fight the charges by contacting the credit agency and disputing any incorrect charge or anything that you just don't understand. You will most likely have to send the credit agency a letter addressing the charge in question. For a sample letter, visit: www.Investitude.com.

4th Send the dispute through *certified mail* so that someone physically has to sign for the dispute and you will have a receipt of the person's signature as evidence that it was received.

What Red Flags should you Look for on your credit report?

The following Red Flags are what you should look for on your credit report:

1. Anything that you can't recall having done.
2. Anything that looks completely foreign to you.
3. Anything that you have questions about.

All of these represent Red Flags that you should look for on your credit report.

What if I use Annual Credit Report (*the free one*) and I can't see my credit score?

Don't worry about it! Not seeing your credit score isn't a bad thing especially if you have the actual credit report in front of you. If you are looking for a solution to knowing your credit score, ask any company that has either extended you credit or denied you credit. Sometimes these companies will be able to disclose your credit score with you after acceptance or denial. Or, contact your bank to find out if they know your credit score. All of these venues will provide you with a free credit score as well.

2 Final Reflections to Consider When Reviewing Your Credit Reflection!

1. **Incorrect credit reports are common.**

Mistakes are often made on credit reports. This is why the agencies that process these credit reports avail themselves so much to consumers. It's because they know that there are oftentimes several mistakes on credit reports and it's not their job to figure out what's correct or incorrect on them. But, if you bring it to their attention, it is completely within their job to fix any incorrect reporting. Bring incorrect matters to the attention of the credit agency so that they will cure any incorrect matters that may appear on your credit report.

2. **Recognize that a misrepresentation on your credit report will affect you.**

Having a misrepresentation on your credit report will still affect you. This may block or prevent you from taking out a business loan, being financed for a mortgage, or other important matters in which having credit is needed.

Please use this information to look at and review your own credit mirror and fight off any distorted credit reflections. I pray that you use this information wisely and that this chapter from me has been able to be a blessing unto you.

A Conversation with the Author:

Swimming or Drowning in Credit Card Debt?

Swimming or drowning in credit card debt?

If you already have a credit card and have experienced what it's like to swim or drown in credit card debt, here are 5 Solutions to get you to the shores of safety.

5 Solutions to get you to the shores of safety.

1. **Cut the card!**

When swimming or drowning in credit card debt, you no longer want to continue to use the credit card, because each time you swipe it, you are hurting yourself more and more. If you have only being using it to deal with your financial emergencies find another way. Instead, don't use it. This decision to continue to use a credit card could cost you dearly.

2. **Organize your Credit Card Debt.**

Next, get organized by creating a plan to pay each company that you owe. In doing so, you may find it easy to simply create a journal in which you record the following information about your credit card debt(s): Credit Card Company name, Total Amount owed, Payment due date, Interest Rate, Company Contact Information.

3. Create a Payment Plan.

Contact each credit card company and reach an agreement to pay the companies back on your own terms with what you can afford (i.e., $10 per month, etc). Please, be honest with yourself by only agreeing to pay what you can afford. Be sure to document any conversations that you have with company representatives by writing their name, date of conversation, time of conversation and employer identification number in your payment journal.

4. Hire a Company to Repair your debt.

Another option is to pay to have a private company repair your credit. Please be sure to do your research on the company before agreeing to hire them to ensure that they have a good reputation for honest and quality work.

5. Avoid Opening a New Credit Card for Debt.

Avoid the trap of signing up with a new credit card company to place all your debt from the other card onto a new one. This is a dangerous game of cat and mouse. Where as the cat is trying to chase the mouse, the dog is really chasing the cat and the mouse is chasing the cheese that it will never catch. Take your time, but don't put it on a new card.

I pray that this chapter from me has been able to be a blessing unto you.

Congratulations!
Now Apply It!

Glossary

Adjustable rates: Adjustable rates are unpredictable rates that vary depending on various factors outside of your control.

Appreciation: An increase in value.

Bartering: Exchanging one good or service for another.

Black: when you have money left over (more revenues than expenses), you are considered in the black, which means you are technically in a healthy financial position.

Business Plan: a written document that outlines the goals of a business and a plan for achieving them.

Collateral: an asset belonging to a creditor (borrower) that will become the property of the lender (usually a bank) if the debt (loan) is not repaid.

Competent: qualified in a field or area.

Compound Interest: when interest earned is added back to the principal and reinvested automatically to accelerate the growth of funds.

Credit Report: a compiled report that includes information such as your bill payment history, if you have ever been arrested, sued or filed bankruptcy.

Depreciate: when something loses value.

Emergency funds: Emergency funds usually refer to at least 3-5 months of income saved or invested conservatively based on your immediate bills and life expenses for emergency use only

Federal Deposit Insurance Corporation (FDIC): Insures deposits up to a certain amount in certain financial institutions.

Financial discipline is simply setting a financial goal that you can set for yourself (i.e. $10,000 dollars saved per year) and putting the time, energy, and resources towards achieving your goal.

Financial Stewardship is keeping track of your money by knowing where it is going.

Fixed interest rate: Fixed Interest Rates are rates that will ensure that your rate is the same for the life of the loan.

Interest Payments: Money gained on an investment by way of interest.

Investitude Budgeting Worksheet – a worksheet that helps you set a budget to reach your financial goals.

Investment Goal: This refers to the ultimate goals that you would like to achieve from your investing such as retirement, college tuition, etc.

Investment Strategy: Plan to keep your investing consistent, effective, and productive.

Launch Party: A type of celebration that previews a new idea, book, business, or other similar novelty and uses it to earn additional money for the project.

Level of Risk: a person's ability to handle the possibility of financial loss from an investment.

Long Term Investment: An investment that is held for over 10 years.

Maturity Date: Specified date that an investment has reached its face value.

Networks: Dependable personal, business, or organizational contacts that you can rely on.

Net Worth: A person's net worth is the total value a person has when all their possessions are calculated such as a home and various other investments like the ones mentioned in *How To Make Your Past, A Blessing To Your Future* minus all the person's debt including the person's mortgage, any unpaid credit card balances, etc. Total Assets minus total liabilities of an individual or company

Private Mortgage Insurance: extra insurance that many lenders require from buyers that make less than a 20% down payment when buying a house in order to protect the lender in the event that the buyer defaults (doesn't pay) the loan. You can usually cancel it once you have paid your mortgage down to the point that it equals 80 percent of the original purchase price or the appraisal value of your home at the time the loan was obtained (whichever is less).

Red: a term of art that refers to technically being a very dangerous financial place where your expenses exceed your income.

Research: Utilizing time to discover critical information that will prove useful in your investing.

Residual income: is having steady sources of income that you can count on to determine how much money you actually make. All forms of compensation received on your payday are considered a portion of what makes up your residual income. Your total residual income is the total amount of money that you actually receive over a year's time.

Short-Term goals: are goals that you would like to accomplish within a year up to five years. For example, fixing the plumbing, planning a summer vacation, paying for your semester of college, save 10% of income

Strategically positioning: positioning yourself with your financial goals in mind means that you are working to accomplish a twofold plan: (1) earning money while also (2) aligning your work situation as a means to accomplish one of your financial goals.

Stock Diversification: Spreading out your investments.

X-Factors: God-given gifts and creative gifts that we can use to earn additional money.

www.Investitude.com

Would you like to get in touch with us?

If you would like some help or assistance in implementing the strategies shared in this book, improving your finances, and increasing your financial knowledge, please contact us for a free financial coaching consultation by visiting the following website:

www.Investitude.com

Once you get to the home page, it will read, *"What is your Investitude? Click here to take a survey."*

Click on the link on the website (Investitude.com) to take the survey. Please answer the short survey questions so that we know what you need assistance with prior to your initial free coaching consultation. At the end of the survey on the confirmation page, it will share a link that allows you to schedule a free 30 minute financial coaching consultation with us.

Need a free app to help you with your finances?

If you would like to use a free app that will help you with your finances and allow you to earn points that can be traded for items, electronics, gifts, prizes, t-shirts, and more, download the **Young Investors App** from the **Google Store**.

Interested in joining Young Investors, Inc. or starting one at your high-school, college, middle-school, or church?

If you would like to become a member of Young Investors (YI) or start a YI Club at your school or YI Chapter at your college, or YI Community Group at your church, please contact us at *www.YoungInvestors.org* to learn more.

Made in United States
Orlando, FL
04 November 2026

90200518R00159